Also by Katara Washington Patton

Successful Moms of the Bible

Successful Women
OF THE BIBLE

Katara Washington Patton

New York Boston Nashville

FaithWords
Hachette Book Group
1290 Avenue of the Americas, New York, NY 10104
faithwords.com
twitter.com/faithwords

First Edition: August 2016

FaithWords is a division of Hachette Book Group, Inc. The FaithWords name and logo are trademarks of Hachette Book Group, Inc.

The publisher is not responsible for websites (or their content) that are not owned by the publisher.

Scripture quotations marked (NCV) are taken from the New Century Version®. Copyright © 2005 by Thomas Nelson. Used by permission. All rights reserved.

Scripture quotations marked (NIV) are taken from the Holy Bible, New International Version. Copyright © 1973, 1978, 1984, 2011 by Biblica, Inc. Used by permission of Zondervan. All rights reserved worldwide. (www.zondervan.com)

Scripture quotations marked (NLT) are taken from the Holy Bible, New Living Translation (NLT), copyright ©1996, 2004, 2007, 2013 by Tyndale House Foundation. Used by permission of Tyndale House Publishers, Inc., Carol Stream, Illinois 60188. All rights reserved.

Library of Congress Control Number: 2016941450

ISBNs: 978-1-4555-3885-0 (pbk.), 978-1-4555-3886-7 (ebook)

Printed in the United States of America

RRD-C

10 9 8 7 6 5 4 3 2 1

This book is dedicated to all the wonderful women I've had the pleasure to journey with throughout life: Mom, Kim, Ethel, Renee, Rachelle, all my super girlfriends and mentors. My life would not be nearly as fun without you.

Contents

Successful Women
OF THE BIBLE

Introduction

Too many times in the world of Bible study, women are relegated to the corners of the story. The matriarchs of the Old Testament and New Testament are not honored or revered, talked about or preached about like the great patriarchs upon whom our faith is built. They are often seen as only wives, mothers, daughters, sisters, or property of our fathers of the faith. But, when read with a different lens—one looking to hear the voice of women—scripture bursts forth and comes alive with numerous accounts of women who made an impact on the Christian faith. These women were not just side pieces to the Judeo-Christian story; they helped to make the story. Their stories and their lives helped to shape our faith—and their stories and their lives can help us live successfully many centuries later.

It's time we hear from them. It's time we learn from these women how to fashion our lives as women of faith. Successful women are in the Bible, and they are still speaking to us today—if we would only listen. Even with centuries of time between us, we can hear the stories of the women of the Bible and emulate their success. Even with cultural differences, we can find wisdom in their chronicles. Even with different opportunities, experiences, and laws, we can sit at the feet of the women of faith who have gone before us and build our stories on their stories. A cloud of witnesses—whether listed in Hebrews 11 or not—can remind us of the power we have when we operate in faith, trusting and depending on God.

We have been fashioned as women by God. We have been uniquely designed as women by God. We have successful models to follow, right in the Bible. This book only looks at a few powerful and exemplary women, but the Bible is filled with the stories of women—some named, others unnamed. When we read God's Word with a lens that seeks to find the contributions of women and an ear to hear their unique stories, we will see the value women provided from the very beginning. Our God is not a respecter of people. *God created human beings in his image. In the image of God he created them. He created them male and female* (Genesis 1:27, NCV). I pray the stories of these women—Miriam, Deborah, Hagar, Esther, the daughters of Zelophehad, Mary and Martha, Lois and Eunice, Mary Magdalene, Priscilla, and Lydia—based on their narratives in the Bible as well as my own imagination, will inspire you.

When we women realize our true value to God, we can then know our true worth and be set free to be all we are created to be: leaders, moms, friends, entrepreneurs, help mates, and most of all women of strong and enduring faith in God. May these biblical examples help us live as successful women.

Miriam

Successful women are joyful supporters and praise leaders.

Then Aaron's sister Miriam, a prophetess, took a tambourine in her hand. All the women followed her, playing tambourines and dancing. Miriam told them:

"Sing to the LORD,
because he is worthy of great honor;
he has thrown the horse and its rider
into the sea."

(Exodus 15:20–21, NCV)

So Miriam was confined outside the camp for seven days, and the people did not move on till she was brought back.

(Numbers 12:15, NIV)

As women, we generally know our girlfriends pretty well. We know who to call when we need some drama—the extra expression and empathy for our situation. We know who to call when we need a reality check and a dose of wisdom. We know who to call when we need an extra pair of hands—and quickly, without any excuses. We know the friend to call when we just want to have a good time or a good laugh without any extra stress. We know our girlfriends and who fits a particular need at the moment.

But among the many types of friends we have, there's a special one I need in my corner more than a few times. I'm sure you need her too. She's the friend known as the cheerleader, the supporter, the inspirational and upbeat woman who will crash your pity party and bring you back to yourself. This woman always has an uplifting and encouraging word, birthed from her genuine optimistic personality and outlook on life. She's the one whose number I have locked in my favorites and ready to dial in a second when I lose my focus, which causes me to downshift my perspective and see more negative than positive.

To make it through this life successfully, we all need a few cheerleaders in our corner. A mother, a girlfriend, a sister, a mentor, a supporter—someone who reminds us that we can do what we set out to do, especially when things look grim and gray and we feel far less than powerful and accomplished and able. Even as women of faith, we need someone who can remind us where God has brought us from and what God has brought us through—right at the moment when we want to give up and throw in the towel.

We all need a reminder sometimes, and we can all use a few relentless cheerleaders in our corner.

That cheerleader in the Bible is Miriam. She's the successful woman from the Bible that I'd want in my corner. Miriam is known as the praise and worship leader and the supportive sister of Moses and Aaron. Her name is sprinkled throughout the Old Testament as her service to Israel is recorded.

Praise Leader

In Exodus 15:20–21, we see that Miriam grabs her tambourine, breaks out in dance, and leads the women of Israel in praise. This prophetess summons the women to forget about themselves and focus on God. She encourages them to sing to God and to lift his name up because of the mighty things he has done. She reminds them to have a great time, praising God for his marvelous works.

This particular praise break led by Miriam comes right after God has performed yet another miracle for the people of Israel. Miriam ushers in this praise service right after the long and dangerous and torturous reign of the ruthless pharaoh in Egypt (Exodus 14). Miriam's people had been in slavery for many years. They had worked hard for the Egyptians and had been treated brutally. Their newborn boys had been marked because the pharaoh feared they'd grow into a stronger nation and rebel against his evil practices (evil always fears strength!). But God had provided the Israelites favor through the midwives who refused to kill the male children—even though they had been ordered to (Exodus 1:8–22).

The Israelites had moaned and groaned and cried out the Lord for help, for relief—and God had heard them. God sent Moses and Aaron to demand that the pharaoh release the people from bondage. Of course, the pharaoh was hardheaded, agreeing to release the people time and time again but then going back on his word. The Israelites had felt hopeless and forgotten.

Then when the Israelites were finally actually released from the Egyptians (after a series of awful and deadly plagues), they faced yet another colossal hurdle: They had to cross a huge body of water known as the Red Sea. And just as they approached the water without a ship, a paddle, or life jackets, the pharaoh was on their trail. He had decided he really didn't want to let the slaves go—who else would do all of that hard work? So just days after being freed from brutal slavery, the Israelites stood between the sea and their enemies. The people had been free for only a few moments, and they heard the chariots and horses of the mighty troops of Egypt behind them.

They felt trapped between water and slavery, between a sea that could drown them and a pharaoh who would work them to death. They didn't want to go back to where they'd come from, but they were afraid to move forward because of the dangerous water in front of them. They felt stuck and paralyzed—unable to go back or move forward. What they knew was behind them was deadly and brutal; what they saw ahead of them was uncertain and seemingly impossible. They faced a tough choice.

But God…

But God commanded Moses to use his staff and stretch it out over the sea; with this one act, God gave Moses the ability to part the sea. The Israelites had a clear path of dry land to walk upon and cross over to the other side. And when the Egyptians followed them, God told Moses to stretch out his hand again and the waters closed back up, causing the pharaoh and his army to drown.

This was a historic event, and Miriam had been a front-row witness to this miracle. She had stood right there with the people—fearful, uncertain, feeling defeated, depressed, frustrated, and hopeless. But God stepped in and did the impossible yet again. Miriam knew this, and she needed the people to remember these details vividly as they faced a new mountain and a new phase in life.

Praise leaders are like that. Praise leaders have great memories, often photographic memories. They remind us of all God has done for us and continues to do for us. With one word or phrase or song, our encouragers can remind us to change our perspective when facing a huge task or a fearful moment; they can remind us of the last time God had to part a sea and make a path, or a way out of no way.

The Miriams in our lives are not just full of hot air and exuberant optimism that's not based on anything sound. The true Miriams in our lives know our story. They are women who will always remain our friends—because they know way too much about us to not be our friends. The Miriams know our secrets. The Miriams know the skeletons in our closets. The Miriams know our praise reports, intimately. They were right there with us through our trials, and they are front-row witnesses in our lives. They've handed us tissues, hugged us tight, held the phone for hours upon hours, and been there during our darkest times. Therefore, their encouragement is real. It is based on what they know God has done for us. They can remind us and paint a picture that pushes us back into a praise moment.

We need to be reminded. We're just like the Israelites. We have short memories. Yes, God just parted the Red Sea in front of our very eyes and did the impossible. Yes, God just brought us through the craziest events of our lifetime and we survived. We didn't know how we were going to make it through that situation, yet we've come out better than we expected—even better than we were before.

The layoff? The breakup? The financial crisis? The test? God got you through it. But now—just a few moments later—there is another issue in our lives and it feels big and insurmountable and problematic. It feels like it can take us out. It makes us want to stop and give up. It's too much to handle. It's the pressing issue on our minds.

It's pretty human to focus on our issues, to complain and let our emotions take us on a rocky path to misery. But Miriam reminds us of what God did yesterday. Miriam comes over to our house with tambourine in hand to remind us of the last time we had a big issue. She refocuses our attention on God's past deliverances instead of on our current issue. She reviews the history for us until we can stand up with her, grab our own tambourine, and do a dance. Oh, how we need the Miriams in our lives. We need them to show up right when doubt creeps in.

Pity Party Interrupter

We all need a good friend like Miriam. She reminds us to take off our garment of heaviness and sadness and halt our laments. She interrupts our pity parties and enters with her tambourine. At first she can get on your nerves. You don't always feel like praising God or remembering all that God has done. Sometimes your present circumstances can trump past miracles, ushering in more sadness than joy, more worry than hope. You don't always feel like looking on the bright side—that takes energy and a memory and discipline to refocus your mind and outlook. Sometimes things are just tough and hard and you want to stew in your misery and use any energy you have left to complain and lament and cry. But that friend who is like Miriam has a way of painting a picture and reminding you of all God has done: Don't you remember the time we were...? Don't you remember the one who got away? Don't you remember the time we did this and should have...? Girl, why are you so worried? Don't you remember what God did last time? Weren't you the one sick and barely able to breathe? Remember that accident? Remember that time...?

Miriam will paint the picture and make you give God a shout, a praise, a clap, your own cheer. Whatever your pleasure, however you praise him, Miriam is right there helping you recall all that God has brought you through. She's the perfect guest to invite to the pity party. She won't let you complain too long. She won't let your attitude get too bad. Why? Because she knows your story, she knows her story, and she knows that God has been and is right by your side.

She Has Two Sides

But just like every human I know, Miriam does have another side. The praise and worship leader is complex, more than a storyteller and a reminder of where God has brought us. She's more than a cheerful presence focusing our attention on God's hand all over every part of our lives. When she's focused on recalling God's blessings, she is at her best. When she is remembering the goodness of God and ushering in his presence, she is the girl we need. But what happens when the praise and worship leader takes her eyes off God? What happens when she lets her mind wander, as we're often prone to do? What happens when she lets just a bit of her humanity take over and relaxes her mind to think of something other than God's goodness?

You know very well what happens. It happens to the best of us. While we know what God can do and has done, when we take our focus off God, evil creeps in and can take us down a trail we know we don't want to follow. Look at what happens to Miriam in Numbers 12:1–16, when she forgets about the many miracles of God for just a moment; see what happens to her when she is not surrounded by others who can encourage her and refocus her to recall God's benefits. She gets sidetracked, and it can lead down a dangerous path.

Miriam grumbles against Moses. Miriam questions Moses' authority, although she has witnessed from his birth his rise as God's chosen leader. Miriam knows the history, but when she takes her mind off God and God's amazing hand in her history, she starts to grumble. She and Aaron sit down and they begin to talk about Moses. Their conversation isn't focused on how good God has been or how God has been with Israel every step of their journey, from Abraham's covenant to Joseph's favor, from slavery days to freedom, from Egypt to the Red Sea. They don't talk about how Moses has been a strong and courageous and humble and fearless leader. They don't talk about how God has used Aaron to speak for Moses and Miriam to usher in the praise. No, their conversation shifts to Moses' wife. *Why did he marry that girl—a foreigner?* And once they get sidetracked talking about Moses' wife, their conversation continues to downshift, and Miriam asks: Has the Lord only spoken to Moses? Doesn't he speak to us too?

Because Miriam, the praise leader, is not focusing on God's goodness at the time, her mind goes down a dangerous path and she wonders why she isn't leading the people. She wonders why her little brother is the one in charge. Hasn't she seen what God has done through Moses? Hasn't she seen the miracles firsthand? Why is she tripping? Why does Miriam suddenly turn against Moses? Doesn't she know his story firsthand and how God had been using him since he was knit in his mother's womb?

Scripture says that Miriam and Aaron talked against Moses because he had married a Cushite woman. Moses' wife was not quite like Miriam and Aaron—she was different; she came from a different culture and a different people. Miriam, the praiser, couldn't tolerate someone different. She let her prejudices get in her way. Instead of embracing her sister-in-law (and even learning about her culture and differences), Miriam started whispering behind Moses' back. This behavior never leads to anything good. We know it, but sometimes we still do it. We are afraid of the unknown and the different, so we talk about it rather than seek to understand it.

Miriam could also have even been jealous of her brother's love. She had been by his side from day one, even intervening to keep their family together, but now he was betrothed to someone else; another woman held his ear at night, and Miriam couldn't take it. Miriam reminds us that we need to get to the root of our issues before they cause us to venture down paths that are not fruitful or good or praiseworthy. We need to get a handle on why we don't like someone, why someone rubs us the wrong way, and why they can cause us to shift our perspective and turn into gossiping girls rather than worshiping women.

It's often a difference or an unknown that makes us wary of another woman: She doesn't talk like we do; she looks different; she acts differently. It can be the fact that we haven't dealt with our own insecurities that makes us jealous of another woman's special relationship with someone we love too. We're afraid that person doesn't have room to be friends with both of us, so we begin to tear her apart. A dangerous web is spun, and we venture down a gloomy path.

I can hear the sad conversation now between Miriam and Aaron—the two who should have known better, the two who should have quickly turned this conversation around and reminded each other of their history, of God's miraculous history. But instead, they continued to look at Moses and his wife and allowed their emotions to take over and usher in negative and unproductive thoughts: *Moses is with that Cushite now. He thinks he's better than we are. He's forgotten that we were right by his side all the time. Look at them talking over there. Why aren't they talking to us? What does she have that we don't have, Aaron? Why has Moses given all of his love to her and forgotten about us? Doesn't he remember that you were the one who spoke for him when he was afraid to talk to the pharaoh? Where would he be if he didn't have you as his mouthpiece? And me, he's even forgotten about me, his very own sister. I was the one who kept him from being taken off to Egypt without his mother. I made sure Mom got to nurse him and take care of him, and now that he has a wife he acts like he doesn't remember all we've done. That woman is no good. She will continue to turn him against us. I hear her people are like that. I know I don't know them, but still—I bet her people are just like that. Look at her. She's different. She's darker. She's just trouble. I think we should lead the people. God hasn't just called Moses to this task. It's taken a team and we are a big part of that team, Aaron. God has spoken through us too. We can tell the people what to do and where to go. Moses isn't the only one with an ear to God's mouth.*

Miriam was suspicious of Moses' wife; she fostered jealous feelings about the woman her brother had chosen to marry. Yes, even the praiser has moments of memory lapse too. Recalling her issue can remind us not to judge ourselves—or her—too harshly, because we are multidimensional. Sometimes the praiser, supporter, and cheerleader can forget how awesome God is too. Sometimes the praise leader can take her focus off God and get sidetracked with the negative and the prejudices and the jealousy that accompanies humans.

And those thoughts can lead to other thoughts, and before we know it, we're in a funk or, worse yet, preparing to do something we know isn't right. With just a thought, we can spiral out of control and into a place we know we don't need to be in. Oh, to guard our thought life.

Wouldn't it have been far better and more prudent for Aaron to stop Miriam before she went too far into this dangerous thought process? Wouldn't it have been more productive for Aaron to return the favor to Miriam and be her cheerleader and take her down memory lane, reminding her of God's graciousness to their people? Wouldn't it have been ideal if one of the women would have grabbed a tambourine and interrupted Miriam's pity party and reminded her how God had been a mighty divider of the sea?

Sometimes worship leaders do not always have the same support from others that they give out. It's at these times that we have to rely even more on our memory and recall all that God has done so we can encourage ourselves, so we can move God's miracles to the front of our minds so the negative can be forced out. When we recognize that we're venturing down the wrong mental path, sometimes we have to speak to ourselves and turn the course of the ship toward our story and our God's goodness toward us. We sometimes have to be our own cheerleaders.

Your Thought Life

Maintaining a proper thought life is vital to being a successful woman. A successful woman recognizes that when her thought life is messed up, her life is a mess. She knows that whatever she ponders and focuses on will shape her attitude and her perspective on life. She knows that when she thinks negatively, she will see things negatively, and each issue that crops up will feel like a personal attack against her. She will go into a defensive mode, striking back and causing distress all around her, all because she didn't interrupt her negative chain soon enough and didn't replace the negative with her recollection of the good, praiseworthy, and excellent reports of God (see Philippians 4:8).

We all need to guard against negative thought patterns. We all need to keep Miriam's story in the forefront of our minds. We need the praise leader Miriam in our corner, reminding us of all God has done. And when Miriam slips, we can't leave our praise leader and encourager hanging when she needs us the most. We should be like Moses, who, even after his sister grumbled about him and talked about his wife for no real reason, prayed for his offender. Moses asked the Lord to heal Miriam when she was punished with leprosy because of her actions. God heard and healed her but didn't take away the consequences; she was still isolated from her people for seven days (Numbers 12:14).

Consequences are real when we fall short. We openly welcome the grace of God, but rarely do we remember that God also sends consequences for sins. We are forgiven and restored, but there is still a consequence we often have to endure when we've allowed sin to creep into our minds and cause our actions to be unaligned with God's will. It's dangerous to slip into that mode, and the successful woman is mindful of her propensity to slip, so she guards her heart and mind even more diligently. She *needs* to focus on the goodness of God—for her sake.

And our consequences affect not only us but also those around us. When Miriam suffered from leprosy, she had to be isolated. She had to be separate from the people. The praise leader could not encourage the people or gather them to sing and dance before the Lord when she was apart from them. Her consequences affected her people. They needed their praise leader, but she was not available. During that time, the people couldn't move for seven days. They couldn't move without their praise leader (Numbers 12:15).

So if you find yourself the praise leader, the worshiper, the pity party stopper, we need you. Don't let your other side get in the way of your praise. As soon as you take your mind off God and all he's done, Satan awaits to creep in and make you prejudiced, jealous, selfish, and so on. All things you'd probably never be tempted to entertain when you're in the midst of praising. James says you can't praise and curse at the same time...so keep praising so you won't curse (James 3:10–11). Keep painting the picture for others to recall God's goodness. We need you; we will stall if you can't get out your tambourine and summon God's spirit to join us and abide with us and remind us to praise.

Miriam, you have an important job to do. Don't let the evil that is crouching beside you get to you. We need your praise. We need your leadership. Keep your focus on God so you can help us recall all his works. We need you to keep moving forward. Keep your mind on the praiseworthy deeds and attributes of God so you can encourage us.

I am Miriam. I am a supporter. I recall all of God's great benefits and acts each and every day. I rehearse them. I repeat them. I remind my sister of all that God has done for her and for us. I remind my family of our story, of just how far we've come. I teach our children about all that God has done. I keep my mind focused on my story, God's story. I won't let anyone forget just what God has done. I am a praiser. I am a worship leader. I dance before God because of all he has done. No one can make me stop praising God. I can't stop. I won't stop. God has been too good to me.

Deborah

Successful women are wise leaders.

Now Deborah, a prophet, the wife of Lappidoth, was leading Israel at that time. She held court under the Palm of Deborah between Ramah and Bethel in the hill country of Ephraim, and the Israelites went up to her to have their disputes decided.
(Judges 4:4–5, NIV)

On that day Deborah and Barak son of Abinoam sang this song:

"Israel's leaders took charge,
and the people gladly followed.
Praise the LORD!"
(Judges 5:1–2, NLT)

Want to see a woman with power? A woman who others look up to and trust and listen to? A warrior? A beloved leader who follows God as she leads God's people?

You need not look any further than the book of Judges, where we meet a woman who showcases exemplary leadership in all she does. I see her as a strong and sturdy adviser, a brilliant leader who takes her cues from God, a woman who says what needs to be said when it needs to be said. I see her as a gentle guide and leader, making her attractive to those needing assistance. Want some advice? Go to Deborah, as many of the Israelites did. Need some encouragement? Find Deborah; she had a spirit that attracted people and made them seek her out for help. Want to be told the truth and not be judged for your thoughts? Deborah was the one sought out for straight talk and truth. All women aspiring to be successful can take a few pointers from the leader in the Bible known as Deborah.

Deborah's story is found in Judges 4:1–5:31. Her story alone can single-handedly dispel the myth that women are second-class citizens or less than—in biblical times as well as today. Deborah is a judge. Judges were Israel's leaders (Judges 2:16) who governed the people after the death of noted leaders Moses and Joshua and before kings like Saul, David, and Solomon were appointed to govern the people. The judges led the Israelites during a time when they were particularly vulnerable to their enemies. Judges were the ones who told the Israelite army when to fight, whom to fight, and where to fight. Judges were the bosses. Deborah was a judge—a noted one, a good one, a fearless leader put into place by God to lead the people during a tough time in their history.

The Israelites, like us, had a history of trusting God for a season and then turning to other gods in another season. They consistently turned their backs on God, got into trouble, and then sought God for relief. The Israelites knew their idol gods couldn't get them out of trouble, yet somehow they kept returning to them. They knew following others wouldn't fulfill or satisfy them for more than a few minutes, but still they kept following the same pattern. Doesn't that cycle still sound familiar?

And right in the middle of the tumultuous history of Israel, we have a celebrated judge—a trusted leader who is also a woman. Deborah is also introduced as a prophet and the wife of Lappidoth. Even during biblical times, being a powerful leader and a wife were not mutually exclusive, regardless of the patriarchal views sometimes presented to us. (Ahh...redemption!) It was and still is possible for women to be strong, valued leaders and loving wives. We can do our work well both inside and outside the home. We can be nurturers who serve our families and advisers who lead our people. Often, the same emotional foundation we pull from to rock a crying baby to sleep can be where we pull from to guide a company, advise a nation, or consult a client. We don't have to separate the two to be successful. We can use our unique design to complement our work and our service. A little nurturing from a strong woman leader can bring out the best in a baby, in a teen, in a man, and in a worker.

Deborah was well respected. Her recorded story begins

as she holds court "under the Palm of Deborah" (Judges 4:3). With a space named after her, she's already gotten accolades usually reserved for the dead. People know this palm to be the place where they can find Deborah. They know this spot to be the place where fair and firm justice can be found. Deborah may not have been allowed in the courts or at the city gates where men rendered justice, but that didn't stop her. She did her work under the shade of a tree. Even when women are blocked—for whatever reason—from serving in positions of leadership, a true leader will always emerge and rise to the top. It's not nearly as important where we lead, but how we lead. When we cultivate our natural abilities and allow them to seep through into whatever task we do, our gifts will make room for us, regardless of our title or station in life. People will seek out a wisdom giver on her job, in the streets, or at her home. True leadership shines through like that.

More Than One Job

As a prophet, Deborah was also entrusted to deliver messages from God directly to the people. Since she is the only judge who is also labeled as a prophet, the roles were apparently different and distinct. You could be a judge without being a prophet. You could govern the people without receiving direct messages from God. But Deborah both led and gave prophetic messages from God to the people.

This fearless leader had her ear in tune to God's message; God trusted her with his message for his beloved people. And the people trusted her to tell them what God had said. She was evidently a bad sister with some serious street cred. When she spoke, people listened. And they wanted to hear her speak. They wanted to follow her advice. They sought her out.

The mark of a true prophet is that what she says actually comes to bear. She's not a fortune-teller hoping to stumble across a common thread in your life to produce a sketchy assumption of what may occur. A true prophet tells what she knows, what has come directly from God, and you have only to wait for it to come to bear. No trickery. No spookery. No special offering, prayer cloth, or charm needed. Just words and actualization.

Deborah was a true prophet: her words came to pass. The bulk of her story in Judges centers around her message to the warrior Barak. Deborah summons the soldier to her tree and tells him what God has commanded: *Go, take ten thousand soldiers to Mount Tabor. I will deliver your enemy into your hands right there.* Deborah is clear; she hasn't embellished God's message, added to it, or taken away from it. She serves it up just as she receives it. This message is from God, and God will deliver the Israelites' enemies into Barak's hands. It's done; Barak just has to go forth in faith and complete the task. But Barak, operating in all of his humanness, needs reassurance. Barak needs some assistance, even though the message is very clear and from God, who has won all of Israel's battles. Barak tells Deborah: *I'll only go if you go with me. I know God said to go. I believe you, I really do. But I need you to come with me.*

And what does a powerful woman and trusted leader like Deborah say to such a request? Does she hold Barak's weakness over his head or run off and make herself a "god" since she apparently has this soldier's complete trust and devotion? Does she try to manipulate the situation and negotiate special favor for herself or her loved ones? No, instead Deborah's integrity shows up and reveals to us what a true leader looks like. This woman agrees to go with Barak, but as a prophet, she must tell him what will happen now that he isn't relying completely on God. Deborah lets Barak know the consequences of asking for more assurance when God has already spoken to him. Barak is not going to get the honor for killing Sisera, the commander of the enemy's army; the enemy will now die at the hand of yet another woman used by God.

Extra Help When Needed

God wants us to believe and trust his word. God wants us to act immediately when we've been given a command. God wants us to trust in him and him alone, not the leaders he sends us, not the signs he sends us, but him. Haven't we seen enough of God's works to believe in God alone? Hadn't Barak seen God's mighty hand in battle before? But evidently God makes some concessions for our humanity and gives us the extra help when we think we need it. In Barak's case, the powerful leader Deborah was his extra help. She prepared him for the victory. She told him how to get ready. She was a supportive leader who knew what Barak needed. So she accommodated his request for her to accompany him in battle.

I can hear her tender, yet firm, conversation with Barak:

Barak, God has heard the cry of his people. He knows they have not always listened to him and have often turned against him to evil, but he is still a loving and compassionate God. God knows his people are sick and tired of being oppressed by Sisera and his army. God knows that Sisera has many chariots filled with iron and that the Israelites are afraid of Sisera and his army. God knows. God hears.

So the time has come for the oppression to end. God will deliver Sisera and his army into your hands. God wants you to stand up and take ten thousand men from the tribes of Naphtali and Zebulun and prepare to attack the mighty army of Sisera. Yes, I know they have those chariots—and lots of them. Don't you worry about that. God has spoken. You know when God gives instructions, things will happen just as God says, right? You know that God has been faithful and has always delivered on his promises, right? You understand the history of our people, right? So, warrior, stand up and do exactly as God has commanded and watch God give you the victory. You can do this—better still, God can do this. Stand up, Barak. Get your weapons sharpened. Call your men and go to battle. God is with you.

What? You want me to come with you? Even though I shared with you exactly what God has told you? Oh, Barak, I understand that you are afraid and want comfort. I wish you could do exactly as God has said, but yes, I will come with you. I will continue to lead you and guide you and help you. But you must understand the consequences.

Because you are asking for a little extra help by having me present, you're not going to get the prize. You're not going to be honored for this victory. Nope, God's going to use yet another woman to get Sisera. You watch and see. God's always got plans, and a housewife named Jael will get the glory here. You see, God can use anyone God wants to, and if and only if they are willing and ready. Are you ready, Barak? Let's go. Let's watch God do exactly what God said and deliver this evil leader into the hands of a woman. God uses women who follow him.

The battle did end with Sisera's death, but just as Deborah had said, Barak didn't get to kill him. Sisera ran to a woman's tent—a woman he thought was on good terms with his people. But yet another woman was at work for Israel here. The woman, Jael, told Sisera to come into the tent and rest. She even gave him something to drink. When he fell asleep, Jael took care of him. (For the gruesome details, read Judges 4:17–21. The Bible has it all!) Barak found his enemy on the tent floor of a woman. Just like Deborah had said, the enemy fell at the hands of a woman. Women show up in the stories of scriptures and in our modern-day stories when our eyes are open to seeing their work.

So the battle was won—perhaps with less glory than anticipated for Barak, but Deborah had already let him know the consequences. Still this mighty woman rejoiced with Barak, and her song of praise (Judges 5) speaks volumes about why she was a successful woman.

Deborah's Song of Praise

Within the first verse of her celebrated song—when she and Barak sing about the victory—Deborah immediately gives praise and honor to God. She doesn't say, *I told you to do this; I am the multitalented judge and prophet of Israel.* No, she says: *Praise the Lord!* She knows where she gets her gifts and skills from. She might be sharp and wise and strong, but she knows these are all gifts from God. She doesn't want the credit; she returns all of it to God.

Her praises are to the Lord (Judges 5:3). God is the one she adores and worships and returns credit to. She continues with a review of Israel's history, praising God for all he has done and continues to do. She acknowledges that God called her to shepherd Israel during a dangerous time when people were not at peace and fled and trusted in idol gods. She says she was a mother in Israel (Judges

5:7), a protective and nurturing guide for the people. She compares her work to the natural and unique abilities of a woman who has borne children.

Sometimes we need the hand of Mama to straighten out our messes. Sometimes we need the nurturing comfort of a woman to set us on the right path. Sometimes we need the firm and truthful words, laced with just enough sweetness that we can swallow them, from Mama to make things better. Women leaders can bring a much-needed soft touch in a cold and cruel world. When we forgo our femininity to better fit in with the boys, I think we miss out on the opportunity to share something most men just don't have inside of them naturally. We can be a woman and a leader at the very same time.

It's no irony that Deborah's name means *bee*; her words flowed like honey, sweet and smooth, yet they were filled with truth, a truth the people needed to hear. Deborah had mastered the art of saying the truth in love, the tough words mixed with the sweetness dispensed from a valued and trusted woman. Oh, to emulate this mighty leader!

Credit to Others

I love Deborah's song. I love Deborah's story. She epitomizes the successful woman. This esteemed woman wouldn't take credit for her amazing leadership that yielded the exact results she foretold. No, when you rely on God for everything, you dare not take credit for anything. It's about God, not you. When you share, you point to what God has done, not what you have done.

When Deborah does give credit to someone other than God, it is to her sister Jael, the housewife who actually killed Sisera. Deborah knows how to salute another woman. With full confidence in God and the abilities God has given her, Deborah knows she is not in competition with anyone. She understands that this battle was won with collaboration. Deborah is just fine with singing Jael's praises. Deborah salutes her and calls her blessed (Judges 5:24).

How often do you salute fellow women at work, at home, in the community? Do you see other women's successes as a reason to celebrate or as a light shining on your own feelings of inadequacy? Do you think women leaders in the community should sit down and spend more time at home? Or do you think women who lead their homes well are weak and have chosen a less meaningful path? Perhaps you are caught in between the decision to be at home more and be in the workplace more. I doubt Deborah would have felt that her work at home competed with her work in the community. After all, she was able to highlight the work of Jael, who appeared to be tending to her home.

Deborah knew that women could contribute in many different ways and in many different seasons of life. Perhaps Deborah had raised her children already or had chosen not to have children because she wanted to be free to share her wise leadership abilities with the people, who she knew needed a trusted leader at this time. Her husband could have recognized his wife's amazing gifts and decided he would be better positioned to be at home and fill in there while his wife served the people. Or she could have hired help or leaned more heavily upon her village.

And, like a wise leader, she celebrated the contributions of Jael, who apparently had a different situation in life. Deborah didn't seem to think of Jael as less than her or even as better than her because she led from her home. No, Jael's contributions were just as valuable as Deborah's— and even Barak's. The mark of true success is recognizing the full array of our gifts as women and celebrating our unique abilities, which are given to us by God to be used to help each other, not to compete against each other.

If we truly see our gifts as gifts from God, we will use them to the best of our abilities, wherever we may find ourselves and in whatever season we are. We will not hide our lights, whether we are in the house or in the workplace. We will bloom where we are planted, showing fruit in the very spot we find ourselves. We will be wise, strong, and filled with integrity, like Deborah. We will speak the truth and follow God's directions, even when it seems hard. We will watch and wait for God to show up and do exactly what God said, because we believe and we trust God. And when the victory is won, we will celebrate. We will sing and praise not because of what we have done, but because we know it is all about God and God has provided all we need to succeed.

Deborah's reign ended with forty years of peace (Judges 5:31), no doubt because of her faithful leadership, undergirded by her unflappable trust in God. The last we hear of Deborah's story is that enemies stayed away and the people lived in peace. This judge and prophet initiated forty years of good life for the people of Israel. Good leadership yields peace. Leaders who listen to God produce peace. Brave and courageous women who don't want the praise for themselves yield peace. Women who know how to praise God and thank God for every good and perfect gift live in peace. I think our land could use some of that peace.

—

I am Deborah. Wise, trusted, respected, in tune with God's voice. I speak the truth in love. I support those who need my help, and I share encouraging words from God. I can be a leader in my home, a leader in my community, a leader in my church— sometimes all at the same time. I know the true mark of a leader is her ability to follow God's lead. I spend time with God, I pray to God, I listen to God, I follow God. And when the victory is won, I give all praise and honor to God while celebrating those who have helped me accomplish our goals. I recognize that this battle isn't won alone. It's a collective effort, and I need and value women from all walks of life who are in various seasons of life. I celebrate women as I celebrate all that God is continuing to do in our lives. I am a successful woman. I walk in peace. Shalom.

Hagar

Successful women trust in God even
when life is unfair and difficult.

The angel of the LORD said to her, "Return to your
mistress, and submit to her authority." Then he added,
"I will give you more descendants than you can count."

And the angel also said, "You are now pregnant and
will give birth to a son. You are to name him Ishmael
(which means 'God hears'), for the LORD has heard
your cry of distress."

(Genesis 16:9–11, NLT)

God heard the boy crying, and the angel of God called
to Hagar from heaven and said to her, "What is the
matter, Hagar? Do not be afraid; God has heard the
boy crying as he lies there. Lift the boy up and take
him by the hand, for I will make him into a great
nation."

(Genesis 21:17–18, NIV)

Even successful women, or especially successful women, know that sometimes life can be unfair, unjust, and downright brutal. Real problems arise. Setbacks creep up at the most inopportune times. Out of nowhere, life can spiral out of control, sending you reeling and wanting to give up. The storms of life can be particularly challenging when they are not prompted by us, when we are truly the victim, chosen by someone else—or something else—to be picked on, messed with, singled out, or cut off. You chose to do right. You chose to work hard, but now you've been slapped with an injustice that feels as if it will crush your life. You feel hopeless, doubtful, angry, sad, and depressed.

Drunk driver—that's not your fault. Fire—not your fault. Abuse—so not your fault. Tanked economy—it's someone's fault but rarely yours. Unreasonable and irrational boss—not your fault, but you need the paycheck. Unexpected death of a loved one who seems just too young to die—not your fault. Expected death of a loved one you are not ready to let go of—not your fault. Watching a loved one slip away from an illness that transforms their minds or bodies—not your fault. Losing a child, losing a business, watching a dream disappear before your eyes— it's tough stuff, real life. How does a successful woman get through it?

We can turn to Hagar for inspiration on handling life when it takes a downward spiral, sending you in search of any way out.

A True Victim

Hagar knows all about living life as a real victim; it wasn't just conjured up in her mind because it seemed like everyone was out to get her. Hagar was really a victim. She was a servant to Sarah (Sarai), the matriarch married to Abraham (Abram). Sarah couldn't have any children—although she knew God had made a promise to Abraham to have many descendants (Genesis 15:5). Sarah apparently believed God, but she wasn't able to think like God or wait on God, so she moved ahead of God in the matter.

A childless and impatient Sarah devised a plan to give Abraham the child God promised him. She gave Hagar, her servant, to her husband to produce a child. Sarah's solution wasn't the most uncommon idea, given the laws and culture of that time. But when you take matters into your own hands instead of waiting on God, you have to be ready to take the good with the bad. There are consequences to every decision we make, and playing like we're God, in control of it all, definitely has its consequences.

So Hagar and Abraham slept together, and Hagar had no problem getting pregnant by old Abraham. But when she was carrying Abraham's son, Hagar changed. Hormones—or the fact that she now had something (a pregnancy) she could hold over her boss lady's head—made Hagar act differently. She started to dislike the woman she served. She rolled her eyes more, talked back, did her work slowly, if at all. Probably looked down on Sarah because Hagar could get pregnant while Sarah evidently couldn't. *I am fertile and you're not. I have the child you've always wanted right here in my womb. Your husband can make a child with me but not with you.*

Unhappy with this turn of events and fed up with her servant's surly attitude, Sarah turns to her husband. *Look at what you've done. You slept with that woman and made a big mess. Now that she is pregnant, she thinks she's better than me. Look at how she treats me and talks to me. I can hardly get her to do anything. You know this is all your fault, right? I just can't live like this, Abraham. I need you to fix this. Now!*

The great patriarch Abraham, refusing to take a stance and remind his wife of how all this even got started, tells Sarah that she can do whatever she wants with Hagar. Abraham just wants peace at home, and he knows he can't get it when Mama is not happy.

Sarah takes Abraham's "advice" and makes Hagar's life unbearable. A woman scorned is truly a force to be reckoned with. And apparently Sarah feels scorned, left childless while she watches the woman she made sleep with her husband traipse around her home with a swollen belly, a constant reminder of what Sarah did not have, that she tried to play God and fix things, yet she still feels empty and barren and terribly unhappy. *How did I get here?* Sarah cries out. *Why is this woman such a trip, acting like she's suddenly better than me just because she can carry a child? I'll make her life as miserable as mine.*

So the woman with power further oppresses the one with no voice. The one who is seemingly in control takes out her frustrations and disappointments and feelings of inadequacy on her servant, the one who serves her. She makes her do more. She makes her work harder and longer under inhumane conditions. She treats Hagar so badly that Hagar's only possible option is to run away.

The pregnant Hagar decides to leave the cover of her home and of her baby's daddy to run away to the unknown. Things were really bad, and staying felt far worse than venturing out alone without resources. She runs to escape the wrath of irrational and scorned Sarah. She runs to escape the silent—and indifferent—Abraham.

Pregnant and alone and on the run, Hagar finds herself in a dry land, a desert. She's depleted. Tired. Angry. Frustrated. Disappointed. *How did I get here, Lord? I was just doing my job, minding my own business. I thought I did everything I was supposed to do. That woman, that awful woman of a boss, told me to sleep with her husband. I wasn't thinking about that old man. I didn't want him. She made me do it. And I thought she wanted me to have this child, his child. I don't deserve this treatment. I don't deserve to be treated like I am nothing. I will just sit here and die. It's better than being abused by that crazy woman.*

When Hagar's despair fully sets in and she realizes that she is truly stuck out in a desert with a baby in her womb and without a job or husband or even caring friend to assist her, she hears a voice. Hagar hears from an angel of the Lord, who tells her to go back to Sarah and to submit.

Excuse me? Did you just tell me to go back to Sarah's house? You must be mistaken. You don't know what I've been through. Let me tell you: Sarah is certifiable. She has no sense. She has no compassion. She's the worst. She's the meanest and cruelest boss I've ever known. She made me sleep with her husband—I didn't ask to. She insisted that I get pregnant so they could have an heir. I did it. I didn't want to, but I did it. Abraham and I slept together, not because I wanted to or even because I came on to him, but because his crazy wife set it up. But when I got pregnant, she treated me horribly. She was meaner than I had ever seen. I couldn't take it. I had no other choice but to run away. I don't know what I'm going to do with this child inside of me. I'm alone out here. I have no one to care for me, but going back to her... I don't think I can do that. It's horrible there. I'm scared. I'm mad and sad and frightened.

The angel was fully aware of Hagar's condition. The angel had been sent by God. The angel knew what was happening, and he didn't leave Hagar without hope. The angel didn't tell her to return and to submit to craziness without revealing God's plan. Her return would not be in vain; her submission to Sarah would not be wasted.

Don't worry, Hagar. I know it seems rough now. I know it's hard to understand how this can possibly work for your good, but trust me, trust God. Return to Sarah. God will take care of you. You will have this child and your descendants will be aplenty. You will be blessed because of this child. Many others will be blessed because of the soul you carry inside of you. Call this child Ishmael. You know why? Because that means that the Lord has heard of your misery. Hagar, you are not alone. God hears your cry. God hears your plea. God sees all that is going on in your life right now, and God will take care of you. Just watch and see.

Another Change

So Hagar returns to the place where she had been mistreated with the promise that God hears her. She pushes out her baby boy and follows the command of the Lord, trusting that God will deliver on his promise. She is obedient and names her son Ishmael. Hagar and her son remain in the care of Sarah and Abraham for several years—probably without much incident. Sarah accepts the boy and tolerates his mother. Abraham is pleased to have a son.

But God is not silent. God's plans have not changed, even though Sarah tried to force God's hand. God promises that Sarah herself will have a child for Abraham (Genesis 17:15–16). So, at the age of ninety, Sarah births Isaac, the promised heir. And again, Sarah's attitude toward Hagar and her son shifts. Sarah has no room for an illegitimate child anymore. She has her golden boy and has no more use for Hagar and Ishmael.

Get rid of that child and that woman you slept with. Our child is here now. I don't want that little boy messing with my precious son. I waited too long to have this child. I don't want that little boy trying to take any of Isaac's rights. Get rid of them now, Abraham.

But this time, Abraham was not so willing to easily give in to his wife. He may have gotten a backbone, or perhaps he was now attached to Ishmael and didn't want to see his firstborn son leave. But God tells the patriarch to release Hagar and Ishmael (Genesis 21:11–13). God will still use Ishmael and make him into a nation—because he is Abraham's son.

Good-bye, Hagar

Therefore, Abraham sends his second family away, but this time he gives them water and food, although it doesn't last long. Hagar again finds herself stranded out in a dry and hopeless place. She realizes that this time she has another mouth to feed. Down to their last drop of water and the last of her resources, Hagar turns from her son, refusing to watch him die. She sits and cries.

Why do I keep ending up in this place? Why has my life turned out like this? I didn't do anything to deserve this. Why is life so unfair? Why me?

And seemingly right on cue, God steps in and sends his angel to speak to a desperate and distraught Hagar.

Why are you crying, Hagar? I told you I would be with you. I told you that I heard you. Don't you remember that's why I commanded you to name your child Ishmael? I hear you, Hagar. Dry your eyes. Things are not as they seem. I know you are hot and thirsty and looking for food and shelter and protection. Just dry your eyes and look right over there. You see it? Just what you need—a spring of water. I've got you, Hagar. I promise. That son of yours will still produce many descendants. They will grow into a nation. Don't worry, Hagar. I will take care of you. I hear you. I hear your cries.

Springs of Hope

In the midst of our pain, caused by the injustices of this world, we can find comfort in Hagar's story. She didn't cause her pain. She was doing her job, going along with her life, when Sarah came up with a grand scheme to move God's hand. Sarah put Hagar into the crazy drama and then turned on her, leaving Hagar without resources. Life can happen just like that. We can be stripped of the very things that symbolize security for us and thrown out into a foreign land that feels much like a dry and unpleasant desert. Circumstances caused by others can send us reeling, searching for cover in a place where there is none.

But just like with Hagar, we are truly never alone—it just seems like we are when we're in our desert moments, feeling worn out, fed up, exhausted, and dried up with no refreshing spring or hope of change in sight. Our past desert experiences, as well as Hagar's, should remind us that God hears us and at just the right time will open our eyes to see the spring, the possibilities that we couldn't see just moments before. God works like that. God shows up in our desperate situations and produces new opportunities, new resources, and a renewed hope that seems like it popped out of nowhere, yet it was right there all along. These types of miracles occur all the time. Successful women pray for their eyes to be opened to view their life incidents as the miracles they truly are.

Our miracles—springs of hope—show us that God can use even the craziest circumstances for our good (see Romans 8:28). No matter who has initiated the madness—and let's be honest, we sometimes do, or at least our attitudes and actions contribute to the issue growing worse (like Hagar's newfound attitude once she was pregnant)—God still hears us and can create a nation, something great and far beyond our capacity alone, from our mess. God can turn our tragedy into triumphant testimonies, if we look for the spring.

Those awful situations can prompt us to look for more or better or different. I know many women who would have never left a job to look for a better one had they not received pink slips. Others would not have ever considered going back to school without losing a job. Many women-run businesses have been founded once a door was closed at a job.

A friend of mine became so ill that she couldn't perform the craft she had honed and perfected since childhood. She thought about giving up at one point, but instead she learned all she could about her illness and now has enough information to travel the world sharing it in workshops to help others, and she's been doing just that for more than ten years. It was not the career she set out to have, but she's touching even more lives than she ever imagined. Her spring of new opportunity came because of her illness.

Another dear friend used the discomfort she experienced at work to pursue doctoral studies, and her dissertation topic was the very issue she endured at her workplace. She now teaches and writes about the issue. She's given me a new twist on a popular quote: don't curse the dark; light a candle, because it will help you find your way.

Your candle, fueled by your God, will show you a new spring and a new opportunity. You will receive a new hope to be better and do something differently. The abuse, the loss, the divorce, the miscarriage, the setback—all the issues you face that made you feel hopeless and lost can be used to point you to a new spring.

Successful women trust in God, even during desperate times. We, like Hagar, need only to dry our eyes, look up, and listen. Listen for God's assurance, listen for God's guidance, listen for God's spring in the midst of the dryness. It takes trust. It takes courage. It takes reminders to keep going, to keep moving, to keep looking for God, knowing that our God hears us each and every moment of our lives. And he will show up—right on time. Have you seen your spring in the midst of dry land? Are you looking? Are you listening? God hears you. Hagar knows as well as every successful woman: things work out when you trust in God (Proverbs 16:20).

—

I too am Hagar, a victim of mess. I too am Hagar, used by someone else to get what they wanted. Mistreated. Abused. Hurt. Left out in the cold to die. But I won't die; I will live. I won't stop; I will hope. I won't give up; I will pray. I know God hears me and I know God sees me. I know without a doubt that God is able and willing to work things together for my good. I've seen it before. I've witnessed it before. God specializes in turning crazy around. I will hope and wait on God in the midst of my circumstances. I will pray and know that God hears and God sees. I have hope in God. I may be down and out, but I have hope in God. I believe every word of God's promises, and I know God hears and sees me. When I am cast down, I look up. When I am treated unfairly, I look to the hills whence cometh my help. I know that God will have the last word and I will be avenged. I don't have to lash out against my accusers or my tormentors. I just have to keep trusting in God. I just need to keep my focus on God. He will direct me and lead me out of this mess. I have but to follow and believe and hope and wait. God will not let me down. God shows up right on time, every time. I know this to be true, and I rejoice in the truth. God is amazing. God is on the side of the oppressed.

Esther

Successful women stand up for a cause.

"And who knows but that you have come to your royal position for such a time as this?" Then Esther sent this reply to Mordecai: "Go, gather together all the Jews who are in Susa, and fast for me. Do not eat or drink for three days, night or day. I and my attendants will fast as you do. When this is done, I will go to the king, even though it is against the law. And if I perish, I perish."

(Esther 4:14–16, NIV)

Pretty girl. Beauty queen. High maintenance. Queen bee. Diva. Prima donna. Cutie.

Society can so easily label women—and we, as women, can so easily join in the label-making and naming game. We see a woman and we immediately conjure up a backstory based on her hairstyle, choice of clothing, and body shape. Just by glancing at a woman and noting her appearance, we think we know her and her story. Our quick summation is usually far from the truth, because most times, what we see on the outside rarely reflects what's inside. MAC makeup doesn't show what we've had to come through just to get to this day. Extensions, weaves, and wigs certainly don't convey snapshots of our character—who we served today or helped yesterday. These outward trimmings also don't tell what we need badly. Nope, they only cover up and present the outward package for others to see and from which many will make a quick assessment.

I bet anyone who would have seen the beautiful, successful woman of the Bible named Esther would have come up with some quick labels too. This woman must have been called all of the labels listed at the beginning of this chapter. She was beautiful. She was lovely in "form and features" (it's written right there in Esther 2:7). She was a queen. She had been hand-chosen by a very powerful king to be his queen. She must have been drop-dead gorgeous. Choose an attractive word or label, and certainly it must have been applied to Esther, the royal beauty.

But for every woman I know, a picture of her beautiful face or body is one-dimensional; it can't even begin to impart her story. It can sometimes belie her true self. As her image sits in an ornate picture frame, you may see her smile and even a twinkle in her eyes. You may see her made-up face and well-coiffed hair, but you can't possibly see her story through that one dimension. And Esther's story—filled with courage and God's providential guidance—is far from one-dimensional, far from being told through a glance at her stunning outward appearance.

A Tough Start

Our beautiful queen Esther was not born into royalty. Her marriage to the king was not some prearranged treaty between wealthy men. Esther didn't grow up in a palace being waited on hand and foot as she received beauty treatments. Esther actually grew up without parents. She was an orphan. Her parents were a part of the Jewish population exiled from their beloved homeland of Jerusalem and taken under Persian rule (Esther 2:6).

We don't know if Esther ever knew of her parents or how they died. Did they run away from her, burdened with the thought of raising a child in a foreign country? Did they die tragically at the hands of their enemies? Or had sickness taken over their bodies and rendered them lifeless at a young age, leaving their precious daughter in a cruel world without a mother or a father?

The woman who would one day become a queen was raised without her mom's words of wisdom. The woman whose beauty would win her favor with the king of Persia was raised without a father to dote on her and look into her eyes and remind her that she could become anything she desired. This woman's story was far from picture-perfect, no matter how beautiful she looked on the outside.

How often are your quick judgments of someone—based on their looks—so far off from reality? What damage do you cause to relationships with other women before they even begin because you've already written their stories in your mind based on their appearance? Do you ever stop to consider that the woman with the most makeup, the most surgeries, or the best hair may be the one who has had to overcome the most? Is her outward appearance so pristine because she's trying not to be reminded of her raggedy beginnings? Or is it meant to distract you from even wanting to know who she really is? Now, some women just come out naturally beautiful and unflawed every single day, and they may not be covering up a thing, but it's wise that we not jump to conclusions based on anyone's outward appearance. The old adage that you can't judge a book by its cover is true for every beautiful woman I know.

Our beauty queen and successful woman Esther certainly had more going for her than her looks, and there is much more to her story than just a royal fairy tale. Esther's gorgeous cover was not indicative of all she had been through or what she would ultimately do for her people. Esther had been raised by her cousin, Mordecai. We don't know if he had help from his female relatives in raising young Esther, but we do know that he was a great guardian and he took really good care of the young orphan. He treated her as his own daughter (Esther 2:7). God can put us in just the families we need—even when our biological families are not available or willing to care for us (Psalm 68:4–6).

Mordecai taught the young orphan of her heritage—even though they were not in Jerusalem but were forced to live in a foreign land among a foreign culture and foreign ideas. He passed her heritage on to her—as she was named Hadassah, a Jewish name. He passed on values of their culture. He must have told her of their history and of their God.

And when Mordecai heard of the rare opportunity for young girls to "audition" for the hand of the king, he seized the moment and deliberately prepared his charge for the contest. I'm sure he told her all that was expected of her; after all, he had been a guard at the palace gate and had observed a lot about palace living. Because a guardian always prepares his or her charge for success, Mordecai told Esther when to speak and when to listen. He told her what to guard against, when to move, and when to remain still. He sent her out prepped for all she might encounter as she prepared to meet the king.

During this time of preparation for the audition before the king, Esther and many other beautiful young girls were taken in and given beauty treatments for nearly one year. Their natural beauty was enhanced even more by the careful care of their attendants. And because Esther was not just beautiful on the outside, her attitude won her favor with the man in charge of the young women (Esther 2:9); he liked Esther so much that he assigned seven attendants to care for her and give her the choicest room and treatments. Can you imagine how good you would look if you had seven people to take care of you for one year—massages, detox baths, deep conditioners, facials, masques, eyebrow threading? We would all look stunning.

Inner Beauty

It was Esther's inner beauty that won her favor and extra treatments. This successful woman evidently didn't let being in the presence of so many other beautiful young women get to her. She didn't let comparisons make her feel less than and force her to belittle others in an effort to get ahead. She didn't try to sabotage anyone else's chance of being queen, even though it was pretty clear that only one would be chosen. No, Esther was grounded. She had been prepared well by Mordecai, and her true inner beauty won her favor.

Because of her internal beauty and disposition, Esther's external beauty was enhanced even more. And isn't that how things work out when you take care of your internal more than your external? When you are happy on the inside and gracious and cordial and pleasant, you look better on the outside—whether you have seven special attendants meeting your needs or not. When we are angry and bitter and fostering issues, it shows up in our face and our body and our health too. No makeup can cover up a displeased and unsettled heart. It shows up right with us and it betrays the front or external look we are trying so hard to showcase. A real beauty treatment begins with the internal and flows to the external. A nasty attitude can make any beauty queen ugly.

But Esther's internal beauty won her favor. It flowed to her outward appearance, and she was chosen by the king over many girls. Now that's beauty! But her story doesn't end with her living happily ever after in the palace. Although she was waited on hand and foot by her servants, her ascent to royalty was not just for her sake, and her character was put to the test during her reign. And this is where her real legacy was left—not in the one-dimensional picture frame showcasing her beautiful face but in the story detailing the history of the people of Israel.

More Than a Beauty Queen

Esther's story as a successful woman in the Bible isn't about her fabulous life as a real housewife of Persia. Esther's people were still in exile—living away from their native land under the control of other peoples, hated by many.

One of the king of Persia's trusted advisers, Haman, had some serious issues with the Hebrews, particularly Esther's cousin Mordecai. Remember, Mordecai was a guard at the king's gate. Haman would see Mordecai every time he entered or left the palace, and just the look of Mordecai got under Haman's skin. Why? Mordecai wouldn't bow down like the rest of the royal officials (Esther 3:2).

The beef between Mordecai's people and Haman's people went back many generations, so much so that I bet neither man knew why their groups hated each other. The fact that one of Haman's enemies would not bow down to him and respect his authority was reason enough for Haman to be angry. (I told you harboring resentment and anger couldn't lead to anything good or pretty.)

So Haman decided to have all the Jewish people killed. Why stop with the one who wouldn't bow down? Why try to get rid of one man when you have the power to eliminate everyone? Haman couldn't just stop at taking care of one person; he had to flex his muscles and go for the entire group. His anger, resentment, and feelings of inadequacy evidently got the best of him. Unchecked feelings of resentment often do; they are nothing to play with and should be dealt with immediately. Seek out a girlfriend, a therapist, a prayer partner, or a journal and get it out before it destroys you and turns you into a Haman, making rash decisions because of one person's inability to do exactly what you say, when you say it, and how you say it. Really? One person? Was Mordecai really such a big threat to Haman, or was it that his ego couldn't handle one more hit? Unchecked anger is dangerous and often results in unreasonable and rash behavior. Put it in check, God's queens!

So Haman, who has won favor with the king, used his favor against Mordecai and the entire Jewish population in Persia. He requested that the king issue a decree to destroy the Jews (Esther 3:9). Not knowing that he was getting ready to seal a deal that would kill his queen's people, the king agreed—not a good look on a leader, not knowing what's at stake (see more about this in *Successful Leaders of the Bible*). But the king ordered the decree, allowing his "trusted" official to go ahead with his plan to wipe out the entire population of Jews living in Persia.

The order was sent out throughout the land, and all the Jewish people feared for their lives. And this is where the crux of the story of Esther comes in. Not once is God mentioned in this story, a fact that makes some view the book as having little religious value. But others, like myself, view this book and Esther's story as extremely religious and a sweet reminder of God's providence, even when it doesn't seem as if God is present.

God's Providence

While God's name is not mentioned in Esther, we, the audience, reader, or listener, can see how God is setting things up and honoring his promise to be with the Israelites—even when they are in a foreign land under punishment. God is present. God is keeping his promise to his people.

Unbeknownst to Haman and even the king, God had planted an advocate for the Jewish people right in the palace. Esther, who was Jewish, although the royal court didn't realize it, would be used as an instrument to save the Jewish people. Behind the scenes, God was setting up a story of deliverance that would loom larger than a battle on the field of war. (Who says God didn't use women?!)

Mordecai still had Esther's ear. He still knew how to guide and lead the young girl who was once left in his charge. When Mordecai showed up at the palace gate in mourning clothes (Esther 4:2–5), Esther heard all about the uproar outside the palace. She immediately sent down some proper clothes to her cousin Mordecai. When he refused to change from his mourning sackcloth, Esther had to find out what was the matter. She sent her attendant to find out.

Oh, dear cousin Mordecai, put some clothes on. Don't you know where you are? Don't you recall just how far our family has come—from foreigners in Persia to officials in the palace? We have found honor and favor in this odd land. You and I are well respected, and we can't take our positions for granted, Mordecai. I am the queen. The queen of Persia. We can't forget just how far we've come—from struggling alone in our little hut to living in the king's deluxe quarters. You are one of his favorite guards! What more could you want?

Don't cause us to lose all the respect we've gained because you don't want to follow protocol. You of all people know that there are just some things you need to do when you are in the palace. Dressing properly is one of those things. Don't come up to the king's house acting like you are a commoner. You taught me to be proper, to take care of myself, and to keep myself up. Now, you do the same! My girls have found some acceptable clothes for you to put on. Go ahead, wash up and stop acting like a bumbling fool at the palace gate. Be respectful. We've been good partners thus far. You got me into this palace, and your information has helped me protect the king. This is a good gig, Mordecai. Get it together. You don't want to go back to our past—wondering where our next meal will come from, do you?

But Mordecai wouldn't budge. *Hadassah—perhaps hearing your real name will remind you who you really are. I've heard from those servants you sent down here to get me to put on the proper clothes and to stop all of my mourning, but haven't you heard what is going on? It's mourning time for Israel, Hadassah. Things have gotten bad, and we need your help. Haven't you heard about that mean old Haman and his plot? He's gotten the king to agree to have all the Jewish people in Persia killed. He's going to wipe us out, Hadassah. If you don't speak up, all of our people could be killed. This could be it for us. But you, you're one of us. You can speak up for us and talk some sense into the king. Tell him how much Haman hates me and why he has done this. Stand up for us, Hadassah. This could be why God has put you in the palace!*

When Esther heard what Mordecai wanted her to do, she was still thinking: *I can't.*

Dearest Mordecai, I hear you. That is so awful what silly Haman has done. I never liked or trusted that man. But what you are asking me to do is unheard of. I know I am the queen, but you just don't understand who we are deal-ing with. No one—and I mean no one—approaches the king without being summoned. Even the queen. I only act when I'm told to act. I only visit my husband when I am summoned. I do what I'm told when I'm told to do it—it's just that simple. Sorry, I can't help. It's just too risky. The king could have my neck for approaching him without being called. Don't you remember what happened to his first wife, Queen Vashti? She lost her throne just because she refused to do something he requested. Now you want me to go in and risk all of what I have gained as queen in the palace and ask him to save the Jews? I could be beheaded for something like that. I just can't put myself out there like that.

You already know that I've been through too much to let all of this go. It's nice in the palace, Mordecai. I have the best food. I have the best clothes. I have people waiting on me hand and foot. And you want me to risk all of that? You know, there was a time we had nothing—literally nothing. And look at me now. I am the queen. I live large in this beau-tiful palace. And you, Mordecai, even you are doing okay. You're a guard at the gate, and you're going to get an honor for your service. You can get in good with the king too. There's no need to start talking about our heritage now. We've passed thus far. Sorry. Maybe someone else can save the Jews.

Mordecai heard the message from Esther loud and clear and he shot back—just as a wise guardian, guide, and mentor would.

All right. Do as you will, Hadassah, or should I say Queen

Esther. But let me remind you that you too are a Jew. When you take off that tiara and fancy gown, you are still a Jew. You can't run from your heritage. You too will get caught up in this war against our people. Don't you think that just because you're living in the king's palace acting like you're not an orphan or a Jew that you will be spared. You will be found out.

It's a shame that you've forgotten whence you came. It's a shame that you are able to turn your back on your very own people. All right. But I know how my God works; if you're not going to help us, God will send someone who will. I just hope you're not caught up on the wrong side when the help comes. Because certainly this could have been a part of your destiny.

You may have been put in this position for this moment, for our people, for our liberation. You'd better think about it. You could be missing your opportunity to bring about change, but I see that your plush lifestyle is more important to you right now. Have you ever stopped to think that just maybe you were chosen to be queen for this moment, for such a time as this, to speak up for your people? Who knows why God allowed you to be in this position? Do you really want to waste your opportunity? You could have been placed in the palace for this time to help God's people. You know God made a promise to always be with our people. You know God has promised our forefathers to make us into a great nation with lots of hope. You know our God has great plans for our people, and you could be a part of that plan. If I were you,

I wouldn't miss out on this opportunity to be used by God to save our people. But do as you will, Queen Esther.

With those words in her ears, Esther came to herself. She transformed from beauty queen—each hair in place, flawless skin, and a tight body—to woman of purpose. She recognized what successful women do: They use what God has given them to accomplish God's purpose. She looked in the mirror and realized that this position and this time were not just about her.

I am the queen of Persia. How did I even get here? I was an orphan, left to the care of my sweet and gracious cousin. Maybe Mordecai is right. Just maybe I've been called for this time to help my people. Maybe God put this into motion way back before I was born. Maybe I won the crown of queen because God knew the Jews would need a strong voice to protect them. God knew that my people would be mistreated and hated and abused, but God heard their cries and sent help. I am that help. I'm not just here to live the fab life in this palace. This is really not about me at all. It's about God's people. I need to take a chance and request a meeting with the king. I have to.

There's no turning back now. I'm going to ask the people to pray and fast—because I need some strength and supernatural power from God. I'm going to get them involved and ask them to send up prayers for me and for our people. Then I'm going to use all that strength to go right to the king and let him know what's going on. He has to know. I have to tell him. This is why I've been put on this earth and in this palace. I know now. I've got to do what I've been called to do.

Prayer and Fasting

Before Esther made her bold move to request a meeting with the king, she understood that she needed some backup—prayer and fasting from the people. Esther knew the importance of backup. It wasn't the armed guard she needed; it was the prayers of the people. She understood the power of praying women. She knew when they got focused, turned down their plates and fasted, and seriously sought God with one accord, things could change. She knew what James would later write: the prayers of the righteous availeth much (James 5:16). Esther needed their prayers; they were her backup, and she didn't want to go into the king's presence without her force.

So she asked Mordecai to get all the Jews to pray, and Esther and her maids also prayed and fasted for three days. When the three days of special prayers were completed, Esther was prepared to break protocol for her people. Esther was set to go to the king without the proper invitation and to reveal the plot against the Jewish people. It was a critical situation, and she stood up and did the unthinkable. Esther broke protocol for her people. She used her influence to lobby for others. And she risked her life, proclaiming: *If I die, I die!* (Esther 4:15–16) as she prepared to approach the king and make her request known.

This wise, prayerful, and now powerful woman put on her finest clothes and stood in front of the king's hall so he would see her. And her beauty did catch his eye. He promised to give her whatever she might want. But Esther didn't jump right in and request Haman's head—she cleverly set things up to make the big reveal. She hosted two dinners for both the king and Haman. Throughout the meals, the king was so pleased, he offered to give Esther whatever she wanted, up to half of the kingdom. (Girlfriend had to have it going on!) After both the king and Haman had filled their bellies and delighted in Esther's presence, the king asked her again what she wanted. And Esther ingeniously seized the moment to make her request.

Oh, my king. I don't need half of this kingdom. I don't want half of this kingdom. All I really would like you to do is to allow me to live—me and my people. Keep the kingdom; it's yours. I wouldn't want to take it from you. All I want is to live. You see, some evil person has conspired against my people. He wants to kill us. Now, if he had just wanted us sold as slaves, I wouldn't even bring this up. It wouldn't be worth it to bother you, o king. We could be slaves. But instead this man has ordered all of my people killed—destroyed and wiped out. But all your queen wants to do is live. All I want is for my people to be able to live. May I just live? May we just live, o king?

This wise woman had done it. She had created an environment pleasing to the king; she had arranged a meeting for her voice and her request to be heard—not just for herself, but for her people. And the king was more than poised to grant her very wish. And oh, the horror for Haman when she revealed him as the perpetrator of such ill intent, right at the banquet table! The banquet he had so delighted in—after all, he had been invited by the queen—would become his final meal. His evil plot would turn against him. His hatred and unresolved issues with Mordecai would lead to his own death. Haman, in the end, was the one destroyed. The Jews were saved.

Who Has Your Back?

When you have a big task, a daunting task, is prayer and fasting your backup plan, or do you prefer to rely on other weapons? Do you know who you can call to get a prayer through for you during an especially challenging period in life? When it is a life-and-death matter, do you call your prayer warriors to seek God on your behalf? Knowing who will truly pray for you is important to living successfully as a woman of faith.

Not everyone takes prayer requests seriously. Some people use them to start a gossip chain. My pastor once said some of the juiciest gossip begins with the phrase, "Pray for Sister Patton; you know she's going through…" We proceed to tell the problems of our sister, getting wrapped up in the details of her trauma, perhaps even forgetting to really pray for her. No, I need the prayer warriors who look and act like one of my friends during those times of need. She says when people ask for prayer, she stops immediately and prays. She's been seen praying on the streets because someone has asked her to pray for them—that's how seriously she takes their requests. She doesn't want to go another minute or continue with her day before she intercedes for that person and asks for her specific need right then and there. Successful women know who to go to when we need prayer, and we know who we can trust to sincerely and boldly talk to God on our behalf.

Those are the types of people Esther summoned so she would have the strength and courage to approach the king on behalf of her people. She knew that when the righteous came together and sought God earnestly, things changed. Esther understood the power of fasting, sacrificing food or other luxuries for a period of time to focus more intently on God and on making requests made known to God.

Like Esther, successful women know when they need extra prayer and they ask for it. Successful women know when a matter is so serious you need to deny yourself for a period and seek God—to fortify yourself, to increase your faith, to build your confidence and courage to do a tough task. Fasting takes sacrifice. Fasting is tough. Fasting means I won't eat or drink certain foods for a period of time because I don't need any distractions. In fact, I want to remember to pray constantly about this subject so I will purposefully go without food or drink to focus on my prayer, so I can intentionally talk to God about my issue and hear a word of clarity and receive strength to do what needs to be done. Fasting is serious. Fasting puts you in another position to beseech God. Fasting puts your requests at another level and takes your time of devotion and prayer to another level too. Fasting causes you to recall scripture you've read. Fasting reminds you to pray more and listen more. Fasting makes prayer a more constant and consistent discipline in your life; your hunger pangs remind you to pray.

More Than You

Esther's story and example also remind us to get over ourselves. We are not called to this life to simply live comfortably in the palace and soak up all the luxuries we can afford. Are you willing to follow Esther's example and risk your comfort to help someone else—especially someone without a voice? Are you willing to reveal your true identity to stand up on behalf of someone else? It can be safe to be a part of the crowd. It can be safe to go along and blend in and cover up who we are and who we are called to be. But Esther is a shining example of all we have to gain when we do step out in faith and muster the courage to use our positions for the good of others.

Do you have the courage, wisdom, and ability to look beyond your own personal needs to lobby for the equality and success of public schools, even when you can afford to send your kids to private institutions? Do you purposefully seek to expose the entry-level student or intern to business opportunities even though you've moved up the ranks, sacrificially sharing your time, resources, contacts, and wisdom? What about serving the least of these, the ones without a voice, without representation, the ones who could have been us had they been given an opportunity or a different set of parents? Are you able to emulate the successful Esther and look beyond your own comfort level and extend yourself to help others in need, or do you turn a blind eye to the plight of those who are not like you?

We have what it takes, right inside of us. If we would summon the courage and pray to God to seek his guidance, strength, and intervention, we could find ourselves proclaiming truth to power and speaking up for those without a voice. We could dig within and find inner strength to do more than sit and look pretty. We could use our positions in the community, church, and workplace to make a difference for others.

Esther's people are ultimately saved. And Esther, in another noteworthy act, reminds us to always remember what God has done for us. She and Mordecai encourage the Jews to remember what has happened by celebrating. They are called to rejoice and celebrate what God has done for the Jews on this day. And to me that's the ultimate act of worship: recalling and remembering and rejoicing in what God has done, not just today but throughout our lives.

To recall our individual and collective histories reminds

us and our children just how far God has brought us. It reminds us of God's providence, how God works in our lives even when we can't see God or even when things look pretty grim. God is present. God is working. And we should always remember.

Yes, Esther's parents died and left her an orphan, but God had Mordecai raise her with courage and integrity and wisdom. He guided her to gain access to a place not normally reserved for her kind. He garnered know-how from the best and gave her a shot at the finer things in life. But it wasn't just for her. It never is only about us.

Successful women see each opportunity as a chance to help more than ourselves. We know we haven't been called to the place of privilege just to live the posh, good life. We've been put in our places—wherever they may be—to shed the light of Christ with our sisters, to help those who do not have help, and to recall just what God has done for us throughout our lives. Each position we have—in our homes, at church, at work, in our communities—gives us a chance to be an Esther in the palace, a courageous voice for the people. This is our opportunity to do good. It's our chance to help the ones we forget about, the ones without a voice or a chance of sitting at the big table.

Have you been appointed to a special place? Are you using your position to enhance your resume or status, or are you looking out for the voiceless? You may sit on the PTA committee and need to stick up for the kid without a tutor or lunch money or computer or tablet or caring mom. Or you may need to be the voice in the boardroom that reminds the policy makers to consider the poor and neglected. Perhaps you need to stand up and be a different voice in the sorority—the one you've been initiated into formally or informally—to show compassion and empathy for the single mom who is excluded, misunderstood, not represented.

Esther held the course and took a risk. She knew she could face death, but she was willing to because she recognized life was about more than her and her comfort. What are you willing to die for? Whose rights are you willing to stand up for no matter what happens to you? To live successfully, we need to follow Esther's model. We all need to look in the mirror and see beyond our physical appearance. We need to see past our fear and uncertainty and see the strength granted from God to stand up for ourselves and to stand up for others. We need to fight for a cause that doesn't just involve us, because life is much bigger than us. Our purpose is much larger than just us.

A successful woman knows that she's more than her outward appearance. A successful woman recognizes that the label on her clothes or the cut of her dress can make her look good on the outside, but she understands that what is inside of her is far more valuable than her looks. Successful women may like their hair coiffed and their nails manicured, but that's the outside. They spend even more time on the internal and what matters—their relationship with God.

Enjoy a massage and a spa day, but relish time alone with God. Tune in with the Spirit of God—sometimes through wise mentors like the Mordecais in your life, sometimes through prayer and fasting—so you won't miss opportunities to make a difference in the lives of others.

Successful women are courageous. Successful women know how to call for prayer and fasting, especially when facing a tough task. Fear may come, but we don't let it keep us silent or paralyze us. Instead, we seek help from prayer warriors because we know the power of prayer and collective prayer. Esther showed us how to act like a queen and live like a true child of God.

—

I am Esther, queen of the land. Called for such a time as this. It's not just about me. I can and will influence and impact others' lives. God always has a plan and a plan of escape for those trapped. I will seek to do all that I can to be a voice for the voiceless and lift up the ones without, sometimes scared, but always trusting in God. I know I have been placed on this earth for more than myself and my comfort. I am able to step out of my comfort zone when needed and declare, *If I perish, I perish.* Why? Because I recognize my mission in life is not just based on me and my comfort. When the cause and need arise, I am the voice, I am the arms, I am the eyes of those who need it the most. I know God is all over my life and is directing my story, so I listen for his prompting and his cues so I might follow. I want to show up at my appointed time to do what I have been positioned to do. I want to be an instrument at just the right time, for the time I am called. My life is bigger than me. My purpose and cause is larger than just me. I want to live so God can use me to help others.

Daughters of Zelophehad

Successful women come together for good.

One of Hepher's descendants, Zelophehad, had no sons, but his daughters' names were Mahlah, Noah, Hoglah, Milcah, and Tirzah.

(Numbers 26:33, NLT)

These women stood before Moses, Eleazar the priest, the tribal leaders, and the entire community at the entrance of the Tabernacle. "Our father died in the wilderness," they said. "He was not among Korah's followers, who rebelled against the LORD; he died because of his own sin. But he had no sons. Why should the name of our father disappear from his clan just because he had no sons? Give us property along with the rest of our relatives."

(Numbers 27:2–4, NLT)

If you're anything like me—a girl child raised during a time when women were finally gaining traction and being seen as capable of doing similar work as men and in some areas surpassing men—you were raised with the notion that you could study or work hard, find a career, and take care of yourself. If you had your education and worked in your field of passion and purpose, you could be self-sufficient and able to accomplish whatever you wanted. Chaka Khan's "I'm Every Woman" blared through your internal playlist and compelled you to take charge and go after what you wanted, because you were every woman, capable of doing whatever needed to be done. You could do it, even if, or especially if, that meant you could do it all by yourself.

Or maybe you were brought up like my mother, a generation earlier. She had a work ethic and attitude that said, if you want anything done, you'd better do it yourself. My mom thought she could do it all too, not necessarily because of her education but because of her hard work ethic and high standards of following through and getting a job done well. She thought she was the only one who could do certain things to her satisfaction.

My mind-set—as well as my mother's—can produce a sometimes blind sense of independence in women. We think we can do it all—and we do. We think we can do things better all by ourselves without the help of others—and we do. We are fiercely independent and strong willed, often opting to walk alone rather than work cooperatively.

But one statement heard at just the right time challenged my perception of independence at all costs. It forced me to evaluate what I might be missing by going it all alone and relying only on myself and God rather than others. A woman raised in Ghana, in West Africa, spoke to a group of women in a mentoring group for young girls. I was present as a mentor, thinking I was gaining information to pass on to the next generation, but I was really getting information to help me pass to my next level of development.

The woman said that as parents and mentors, we move children from dependence to independence, but then we have to teach them interdependence. I heard her wisdom at just the right time in my life. I had to reevaluate my stance on independence and doing life solo (or even with just my own chosen clan), and start to see my life through community and with others (regardless of my marital status). I needed to learn that depending on others was not a sign of weakness, but interdependence could actually make me and others stronger. I could gain from my mentees, who were much younger than me and who I assumed needed me more than I needed them. I could grow from just showing up and helping others, being connected to a community. This interdependence served as a link in a chain. It connected us, making us stronger together than we were apart.

And there's a group of women in the Bible whose interdependence changed the history of a people and further inspires an independent gal like myself to value interdependence even more than independence.

Their Interdependent Story

The daughters of Zelophehad, as with most of the women during biblical times, lived during a time when women were just an extension of men—their daddies and then their husbands. Women had no right to own land; after all, they too were seen as property. A donkey couldn't own land, so neither could a woman. What would she do with it? Thank God, you've come a long way, baby.

Zelophehad, a man who belonged to the tribe of Manasseh (Joseph's son), had only five daughters (Numbers 26:33). He didn't have any sons to leave his land or inheritance to. Zelophehad's five daughters' names—Mahlah, Noah, Hoglah, Milcah, and Tirzah—are recorded and repeated three times in scripture. They have a place in history.

Their dad, Zelophehad, died in the wilderness and didn't have any sons who could inherit his land. Under the law, his name would go without being recorded when his land was given away (Numbers 27:4). Basically, when Zelophehad died, so did his legacy, according to the law at the time.

But these fierce women didn't think this was right, and they wanted something done about it. Don't you love them already? They didn't just sit around and have a hen party and complain about how awful the law was or how cruel and disrespectful those men were. They didn't scream from their rooftop and write a nasty note about

Moses and the leaders. They didn't even turn against each other—deciding to fight for only themselves instead of with each other, conjuring up reasons why one should get the land over the other, pointing fingers at who had done the most work or who deserved it more than the others. No, these mighty women decided to stand up for themselves, together. Can you hear their special meeting to discuss their plan of action?

Okay, girls. We're about to lose everything we ever had. Our dad's name is about to be wiped out from the records. We could be sold into marriage or left homeless and left to fend for ourselves. Who knows what will happen then? But we have a choice. We can come together and stand right at the doorstep where Moses and those guys meet. Let's put aside our bickering for now; let's look past our differences and our issues and pull together. We need each other right now, and making our request known to Moses together is way more important than us acting independently.

It will take some guts. What we're asking for is unconventional. Land has never been distributed this way before, but we have no other choice. Let's work together to see what can be done. This means we're all going to be a little uncomfortable at times. You know the oldest, who likes to boss everyone around, will have to listen sometimes. And the baby, who always thinks she's being picked on, is going to have to put on some tough skin and get over her feelings. And the middle girls are going to have to speak up. It's about the group, not individuals. We can fight about our issues later, but for now, we've got to come together. We need to be on the same page to approach Moses and get our rights. Y'all ready? All for one? One for all? Let's go!

So the daughters of Zelophehad showed up and stood tall and spoke to Moses, Eleazar the priest, the tribal leaders, and the entire community at the entrance of the tabernacle (Numbers 27:2). Everyone was there. These women were tough. These women were fierce. I adore these women. I admire them. I need to be more like them.

Their spokesperson cleared her throat and adjusted her crown and declared: *Our daddy died. He wasn't a part of the group that rebelled against the Lord. What he did was his own doing. But he didn't have any sons. He just had these lovely daughters you see here today. So let us ask you: Why should our father's name disappear from the clan just because he was able to give birth to girls and not boys? Does this seem fair? Really? We want the land. Give us the property along with the rest of our relatives.*

Not Only about Us

These five women were not just standing up for themselves or even their father's name; they were looking out for their other relatives. These "others" could have been their mom or Zelophehad's sisters or anyone else. They didn't just look out for themselves. Unselfish, bold, able to work together—the list of admirable qualities keeps growing as we keep reading about this buried treasure called the daughters of Zelophehad.

And sure enough, Moses took their case seriously and brought it before God. Isn't this where we really should bring our cases? God, the great judge and administer of justice, heard Moses and declared that the daughters' claim was legitimate (Numbers 27:7). They had a point. The law was not fair, and these girls should have the land and so should their father's other relatives.

Then God gave Israel a new rule to follow for men who died with daughters and no sons (Numbers 27:8–11): If a man doesn't have sons, then his inheritance should go to his daughters. Because of the fierceness of these five women, the law was changed. Because they stood together, future women would be protected and cared for even if sons or husbands or other men were not around to care for them. Their story had a point. Their story had a meaning. It's not haphazardly thrown into scripture; it's not an aside. Their story is a part of Israel's history and a part of our Judeo-Christian history. These women represent us. These women show us how to pull together and get a job done for others.

What keeps us from coming together as women like the daughters of Zelophehad? So many things. Different personalities, different methods, different ideas, different backgrounds. But don't you think these five women had five different personalities? And they were sisters too. They lived closely together having to deal with parental favorites, chores, and birth-order issues, and yet, they still got over all that, or at least put it to the side for a moment, to come together for a great cause.

When was the last time you looked beyond your differences with a sister—personality, background, sibling rivalry, marital status, race—and decided that your cause was bigger than your differences? What you and others stood to gain was so much greater than your idiosyncrasies or the things you just couldn't stand about another sister. It's not always easy to work together, but these women prove that it is worth it.

The daughters of Zelophehad show us that there is power in numbers, and there is gain when we sacrifice our own thoughts and push past our issues and come together. We can do so much more, not only for ourselves but also for others.

What sister do you need to cut some slack today so you can get along, at least temporarily, and work together? Which sister do you need to look past the way she dresses, talks, believes, and so on, so you can put your heads together and stand as a united front and fight for a change in your home, in your community, in your church, wherever it may be? What past offenses do you need to let go so you can focus on what's even more important? How do you stop petty differences from blocking the bigger vision? How can you learn to focus on your common goal rather than on your pesky differences? How can you forgo some of the comforts and ease of walking alone to pull together?

I don't want my personal differences to stop me from doing something greater. I know I am one person, and the daughters of Zelophehad teach me that I can do much more with more women. I know it's difficult. I know it takes patience. Ever try to arrange a time to meet with sisters and think to yourself, *It would be easier to just do this alone*? Calendars conflict, times (and time zones) don't match, places to come together are not always in the midpoint, so I have to go an extra mile.... It takes effort to come together. But according to the outcome from the daughters of Zelophehad's story, it's worth it.

I once trained for a marathon. Before you get impressed, I must share that I actually walked most of the marathon, and the real reason I signed up for it was because it was in Bermuda, a place I wanted to visit. So I got sponsors and my company's match and committed to walk 26.2 miles...geez! But the training was great, and it really prepared me for the marathon.

Every Saturday a group of committed people met at the lakefront to walk or run or walk/run a set number of miles. When we started doing double-digit-mile walks on Saturdays, it started getting cold in Chicago. It took more and more motivation to get out of my warm bed and drive to the lakefront to walk eighteen miles. Because I wasn't sure I'd walk the entire marathon, I did run a bit, but not very much. So I didn't often have a mate during those walks, because either the runners were too fast for me or the walkers were too slow. During one of those particularly rough mornings, I told myself, *If you need a partner this morning, you may have to slow down, but you'll have someone to walk with you, and it will make the walk more tolerable, and you just may be able to finish.*

I made it that morning, and I completed that crazy long marathon in crazy hot Bermuda. Not because I'm some great athlete (far from it) or because I am so determined and goal-oriented (not always the case), but because I walked with a crew of women who laughed and talked and cheered each other on. I could probably have walked faster, but I chose to be in community with women that day. I needed them more than I needed to finish a few minutes quicker. Let's face it, I was far from winning any money for this race.

The sacrifice of slowing my gait was worth it, and the accomplished feeling of finishing reminded me that some goals are better shared. Some goals are better attained in community. Is it easy? Nope! Does it require more patience? Absolutely. But it is so worth it.

Before you give up on a group of women—or one woman—consider the daughters of Zelophehad. What would have happened if they had not been able to come together and approach Moses, who in turn beseeched God? What if they had looked out for just themselves and not their father's other relatives? Would a law have been changed? Would countless other women have gone without rights, without land, without protection?

We won't know, thankfully, because those women stood

together in solidarity, pushing their issues to the back so the common good could rise to the top. I like those women. They inspire me. They are every woman!

———

I am the daughters of Zelophehad. I join in solidarity with women across the world. I know we are different. I know we have different backgrounds and experiences and personalities. I am well aware of our differences, but I also know how powerful we can be when we unite. I am a daughter of Zelophehad, and I join hands with my sisters to collectively raise our voice and change injustices. Our fight is not only about ourselves; it is also about our other sisters and our legacy. I want to make a difference, and I don't want to do it alone. I want to contribute and play with the band of sisters making a difference in this world for myself and for others. There is power in numbers. It's worth overlooking our differences and forging ahead, together.

Mary and Martha

Successful women can complement each other.

While Jesus and his followers were traveling, Jesus went into a town. A woman named Martha let Jesus stay at her house. Martha had a sister named Mary, who was sitting at Jesus' feet and listening to him teach. But Martha was busy with all the work to be done. She went in and said, "Lord, don't you care that my sister has left me alone to do all the work? Tell her to help me."

But the Lord answered her, "Martha, Martha, you are worried and upset about many things. Only one thing is important. Mary has chosen the better thing, and it will never be taken away from her."

(Luke 10:38–42, NCV)

Sometimes working with women can be challenging, to put it mildly. Even after discovering the victorious and

inspirational account of how the daughters of Zelophehad put aside their differences and rallied together to cou-
rageously approach Moses and the elders to change the
laws that only provided an inheritance to male heirs, I
still have to think twice and pray without ceasing when
joining a volunteer committee at church or school, pur-
suing new friendships (and keeping old ones), or uniting
with a female-dominated group. Working with and even
playing with my beloved sisters and girlfriends can create
tension. In all of our gloriousness, we embody an eclec-
tic band of circumstances, viewpoints, personalities, and
emotions. Just ask anyone in a sorority or other all-female
group, office, or choir. It can be tough for women to come
together—even for a worthy cause.

I once heard a speaker at a women's conference say that
being in a relationship with any other woman is akin to
two porcupines trying to hug. We want to be close, we
want to love each other, we want to work together, but
those prickly quills of ours get in the way as we reach out
to extend ourselves. And how else will porcupines hug if
they don't bring their quills? These defense mechanisms
are a part of what makes porcupines porcupines. They
would not be porcupines if they did not have quills, which
also protect them from dangerous predators. Yet they can-
not hug without pricking each other. Quills are inherently
a part of these animals, much like our personalities, experiences, and emotions are all a real and essential part of
us. And just as our very being shows up every time we go

to hug, our nature shows up when we join forces to work together. It's not realistic to expect anything other than who we are to show up when it's time to get together. It's not fair to expect someone different to show up. After all, doesn't a successful woman live authentically as herself, wherever she may be?

I'll go ahead and name the issue we have when coming together, because I love women, I am a woman, I know women, and I've had challenging relationships with women: We are emotional and passionate and hardworking and caring and chatty and so much more. When I've poured my soul out to my husband, there are times when he's stared at me like a deer caught in the headlights and sincerely pleaded: *Call your girlfriend*. I chuckle sometimes. I get it now. There are some conversations better reserved for my female compadres. There are some topics better discussed with every ounce of emotion and empathy and compassion only a sister friend can muster up. Sometimes I need the complex mind and heart of my sister, and sometimes I simply prefer the complex mind and heart of a woman to talk to and to work with.

And, if we are continuing to be honest, we will admit that women know how to push each other's buttons. We know just the word to utter, the facial expression to reveal, or the gesture to make to garner a desired reaction or emotion from another woman. The same things that make us great friends, confidantes, empathizers, ride-and-die chicks are also what make our relationships more complicated. We carry our emotions on our sleeves a bit more, and that can be good and bad. I want to be free to share my emotions and how I think. I don't want to compartmentalize my life and not have my feelings flow, but I am objective enough to know that that causes issues, especially when my sisters gather.

So how do we do it? How do we come together to produce more than we can alone? A closer examination of two other sisters in the Bible, Mary and Martha, can show women how to work together, even with our different personalities, gifts, and skills.

Friends of Jesus

Mary and Martha were sisters who lived in a village outside of Jerusalem. These women, along with their brother Lazarus, were considered friends of Jesus. Scripture records Jesus visiting the family several times during his ministry.

On one particular visit, these two women's distinct personalities clashed, and one sister, Martha, couldn't keep quiet about it. Martha, the fireball of the duo, was busy serving Jesus and his friends. She wanted everything to be just perfect. You know the type. She broke out the fine china and linens. She dusted off the chandeliers and other hard-to-reach places because that's what you do when company comes. This talented hostess cooked up her best meal and Jesus' favorite dishes. She knew Jesus was an important guest. She knew Jesus had been traveling around the land trying to get the people to understand what God was doing through him, and she wanted him to feel rested and refreshed in her home. She was being a great hostess. She was taking care of her most revered guest.

But as Martha pulled everything together for the smashing dinner, she glanced over into the living room where everyone was gathered at Jesus' feet awaiting the next parable or teaching he'd dispense. This group also understood Jesus' significance, and those gathered at his feet wanted to soak up every moment they could with him. As Martha looked at Jesus' followers huddled in the living room, she saw her sister Mary, right there front and center at Jesus' feet. Mary was sitting down, enjoying the presence of Jesus. She listened carefully and delightedly to each word as it fell from his mouth.

Mary's place at Jesus' feet didn't sit well with her sister, however. I can hear Martha clanging pots together in the kitchen and mumbling right now: *Is that Mary sitting down right at the feet of Jesus? Does she not realize all the work I have to do in this kitchen? Why does she get to sit down and rest? That girl is lazy. She better get up and help me. She lives here too. I shouldn't have to do all this stuff by myself. I'm going to get her right now.*

Martha rushed into the living room, but interestingly she didn't grab Mary and demand that she come to the kitchen to help. Instead Martha went straight to Jesus, the honored guest, whose authority was clearly recognized by both women. Martha appealed to Jesus to make things right: *Lord, don't you care that my sister has left me to do all the work by myself? Tell her to help me!*

And in all of his wisdom, seeing right into what women would need to hear even today, Jesus replied, "Martha, Martha, you are worried and upset about many things, but only one thing is needed. Mary has chosen what is better, and it will not be taken away from her."

Jesus gave a message to Martha and to us. Choosing to sit at Jesus' feet, even when there is plenty of work for you to do, is always the best thing. Choosing to stop and soak up the beauty of having a visit with Jesus always trumps a great meal. Choosing to listen to the teachings of Jesus and rest in his presence wins over busywork and important work, every time.

Yet Jesus didn't say that the meal wasn't important or even needed. I'm sure he enjoyed Martha's cooking like everyone else, and I'm sure he was happy to have a good meal. But Jesus valued and thereby encouraged us to value more than physical food. Jesus encouraged us to care for more than the physical and to value the spiritual. He didn't tell Martha to sit down and stop cooking (he probably wanted to eat too), but he did commend Mary for her position in his presence. Mary was soaking up the spiritual, and that was valued, that was needed, that would not be taken away from her.

As women, we also have to realize that there is more than one way to serve; there is more than one way (our way) of accomplishing any goal. For Martha, serving Jesus meant putting on the best dinner for him so he could enjoy himself and nourish his physical body. For Mary, serving Jesus meant sitting at his feet and hearing his words. It would later mean pouring expensive oil on his feet, which essentially prepared him for his sacrificial death (see John 12:3–8).

The Comparison Game

As women work together, we can't forget our common goal. Mary and Martha both recognized Jesus' authority and understood what an honor and pleasure it was to have him in their home. Martha couldn't see the value in Mary's service at Jesus' feet. Martha could only see and feel that she was busily working while Mary was just sitting.

Isn't that how it always seems when we take our eyes off our goal and glance around at other women we're supposed to be working with? We start to compare what we're doing to what it looks like others are not doing. We start to list all we've done and compare it to the "little" she's done. Instead of making our part the best we can, we complain about what someone else is not doing. We're better off if we focus on our gifts and skills, hone them, work them for good, knowing and believing and trusting that our sister is doing the same with her gifts. It looks different. It comes off differently, but together, the goal—to honor our guest—can be met. Just as the body is made up of many different parts with various functions (1 Corinthians 12:1), women who work for a common goal have different functions. Each part of the body may do something differently, but it is still very much needed.

As we work together with our different gifts, we have to guard against the nasty comparison game, because it never leaves us in a productive place. It makes us whiny and self-focused, and it thwarts our own ability to do our best. I see the issue when Martha speaks up because I know this issue. I suffer from this issue myself.

It doesn't seem fair that I'm the one in here doing all this work. Why does she get to sit down on her butt and just listen to Jesus and enjoy the company while I'm sweating over the stove and making sure everything is all right? Jesus, tell this girl to get up and help me. Can't you see I need help? It's just not fair. Little Miss Mary is sitting down. She looks way too comfortable to me.

Sure, I'd like to hear all that Jesus has to say—he tells some pretty good stories—but who will feed all these people? Food doesn't just cook itself. This house didn't just turn into a fabulously clean place by itself. It takes some work to get all this stuff done, and I'm tired. I'm tired of doing all this work alone. Why does Mary think it is okay to sit back and enjoy Jesus while I work? Who does she think she is—one of the guys? She's not Lazarus or Peter or James. She's a woman, and she belongs in the kitchen right next to me. It's not fair. It's not fair. It's just not fair.

When we compare our actions to anyone else's, we will get a lopsided view of things. We can only see from one vantage point. Martha is tired, and she is busy. Nothing anyone else does can compare to what she's doing and feeling at the time. So Mary's valued place right in Jesus' presence is not seen as such; it's seen as Mary just sitting down and not working.

A successful woman guards against comparing herself to another. I know I can't measure what I'm doing against another's gift. What I'm doing—if it is my gift or calling or what I've agreed to do—may come naturally to me. It might even be easier for me to do this than for anyone else to do it. I've been designed to handle the particulars of my gift. I understand and can bring my unique makeup and experience to accomplish my designated part of reaching our goal.

Likewise, I don't always know the value of another's work just by observing it. To the naked eye, she could just be sitting down, like Mary seemed to be. She could be cleaning up or organizing or making flyers on the computer or having lunch with a potential sponsor, which are all important tasks, but I can't see how that will contribute to our goal. I only know what I'm doing and how tired I am. I can't see how she may be used at the eleventh hour to finalize some important component; I only see her sitting down, looking like she's enjoying herself, while I am stuck here doing all of my work and comparing our actions.

It's far better for each of us to work and live within our calling and gifts, to work to the best of our ability and as unto God (Colossians 3:23). And leave my sister be if she is working and living in her area of expertise. If we all do our part, whatever that may be, we will be better off and our mission will be accomplished.

In order to be together, the porcupines have to know and expect to get pricked. They expect it and work around it and prepare for it. But when hugging is more important than the annoying prick, they join forces and unite. When we need and desire to be in community with our sister, we learn to accept her pricks and her different contributions to a project; we embrace her different viewpoint and personality; we value her unique contribution in our lives.

Better Together

When you grow weary of working with your sister, which is expected, try changing your focus. Instead of highlighting your differences, focus on the sum total of combining your efforts. When we put action, like Martha, and devotion, like Mary, together, we gain more than just one alone. When we put confrontation and compassion together, we can get things done with love. When we match the creative with the practical, we get the beautiful completed on time. When we combine the loud and the quiet, the boisterous and the serene, the brass and the string, we get an orchestra filled with different sounds that create melodies for the soul.

I want to play music, but my solo is not good enough. I want to be a part of a beautiful sound that touches lives and inspires others, not just sing a single song alone. When I recall this, I can handle women who think differently. When I remember that my sister is gifted differently, I can appreciate her gifts and see her quills for what they are. It will take some practice and some maneuvering, but I can come together with her. I may get poked a few times, but our mission will be worth it. I need my sister. She's not like me, but I need her. Because she is not like me, I need her.

—

I want to appreciate the Marys in my life, and I want to value the Marthas in my life. We may be different, and we may have different gifts, but we can work together. I can give my fellow porcupine a hug. It might prick, but it will be worth it. If we all allow each other to operate in our own gifts, to be ourselves and flow, we will get much more done. We need the prayers, we need the contemplative, and, yes, we need the fiery, hard women of action. Both/and, not either/or. We're not working against each other; we are working together. Our focus should be on the main thing and let it flow. It won't always seem fair, but it can work.

Lois and Eunice

Successful women influence the next generation.

I remember your genuine faith, for you share the
faith that first filled your grandmother Lois and your
mother, Eunice. And I know that same faith continues
strong in you.

(2 Timothy 1:5, NLT)

What will people say about you when you are gone? What
will be your legacy? Will you be remembered for a particular act or action or personality trait? Will you be remembered for what you sowed into the life of someone else—a
child, a group, an elderly person, a coworker, or a class?
Will anyone look back on their time with you and say, *She
impacted my life; she made me think about something differently or see something in a new way*? Or will you be forgotten as soon as your body is placed in the ground because
you didn't impact anyone; you merely existed and took

up space on this planet? You lived your life for you and you alone, not creating a ripple in the pool or stirring up anything that might cause a mess, living safely and cautiously as your time ticked away, forgetting the risks to keep the peace, refusing to sacrifice security or comfort to raise your voice and be heard on behalf of someone else—or even yourself.

I don't think anyone ever says, *I want to just leave this earth without adding an ounce of value to anyone's life. I want my time on earth to be erased as quickly as I'm gone.* No one admits to wanting their life to be in vain, lived only for the moment or only for themselves—at least not anyone who has passed their teenage years (and I even know some teens who have already changed others' lives).

But how do we leave an impact on others? How can our lives be more than just fading timelines or monotonous routines filled with crossing off tasks on a never-ending to-do list? How do we muster the courage to extend our reach and touch a life besides our own? How do we live our lives as more than just a given time period to tick off items on our bucket lists? And isn't living really about touching others, sharing with others, being in the company of others? Successful women already know that the isolated life can be lonely and insignificant, although if you're anything like me, you still grapple with how in the world you can make an impact on someone else's life when you don't even have enough hours in the day to attend to your own personal needs.

In 2 Timothy 1:5, two women are remembered for their legacy, which influenced a young man who ultimately impacted our Christian faith many, many years after they lived. These two successful women are Lois and Eunice, and they are esteemed for passing on their faith to their grandson and son, Timothy. These two women, mother and daughter, are engraved in history as faith-filled women who not only believed and trusted in the God of Israel, but also showed Timothy, who assisted Paul in setting up early churches, how to live.

Faith Is Meant to Be Shared

Faith isn't just for us. It's not just our insurance to get into heaven and live eternally. Faith is to be shared and shown and used as an example to light the path for others. In fact, if our faith is genuine, truly connected to the belief that God loved us so much that he sacrificed Jesus for our sins so that we might have both eternal and abundant life (see John 3:16 and John 10:10), then we want others to know about the God we serve. We want others to experience the sometimes unexplainable love we have received from God. We want others to know how to lean on and depend on and trust God for everything. Faith is something we want to share. We want it to be contagious, spreading to the lives of those around us.

I'm not sure what Lois and Eunice taught Timothy

exactly, but they had to have powerful impressions on the young man, for even his mentor, Paul, saw it and knew that he had been in the presence of faith-filled women. Was it the early-morning audible prayers or late-night singing? Was it how they handled a trial that came up and relied solely on God to bring them through? Was it the scriptures they read over and over to Timothy as he grew up and then lived out in front of him so he'd know? It was probably a combination of all the things these two women did in their everyday lives, reflecting their love of God and their care for Timothy.

While Lois and Eunice are lauded as faithful women who shared God with Timothy, we don't learn about how Timothy's father influenced him. Timothy's father is mentioned in Acts 16:1 and is said to be Greek. In the same verse, Timothy's mother is said to be a Jewess and a believer. Her faith in Christ is noted, but Timothy's father's faith is not mentioned. Presumably, he had not converted to Christianity, or perhaps he didn't display his faith as strongly or certainly as Eunice. He may not have signed on to follow the example of Christ and become a convert to the early church. He may not have believed in the miracles of Jesus or the teaching reminding us to love one another just as we love ourselves. Perhaps Timothy's father wasn't convinced of the resurrection and the power available to believers through the Holy Spirit.

Or Timothy's dad could have been like some modern

men: He didn't display his faith or talk about it or speak the same language as women. Perhaps he believed deep in his heart, but he didn't talk about Christ or go out of his way to share his faith, even with his son. He could have considered faith as private. He could have displayed little or no emotion about Christ. Either way, scripture is silent about his faith, and Paul uses the example of faith displayed by the women in Timothy's life to encourage a young Timothy.

I pray any records of my life do not leave out my faith. I want faith to be such a major part of my life that you can't talk about me without talking about my faith in God. I want the lines of my story to recollect my faith and how I passed it on to others without leaving a question in anyone's mind.

But regardless of where Timothy's father stood in his faith, it apparently didn't change or lessen the faith of Eunice, his mother. She faithfully passed along her trust in God to her son. She showed him the way and poured her faith into his life in such a manner that she is remembered by Paul.

I can overhear a disagreement she has with her silent-in-the-faith husband now: *Eunice, dear, why are you always telling that boy about Jesus and his miracles? Let him be. You don't want him to grow up being soft and wanting to just sit around the kitchen listening to stories you and your mother tell. If he will be a Christian, he will be a Christian. You can't pass on your faith to him. It's a personal decision. Just let him be, will you?*

My dear husband, you just don't understand, do you? I don't talk about Christ and share with others and love like this just by chance. I have had an encounter with Jesus of Nazareth. I may not have been here when he walked the earth, but I've been changed by him. Once I grasped the great sacrifice Jesus made for me and then began to realize that my faith in Christ gave me power—the same power that actually got Christ up out of the grave—I couldn't remain the same. I couldn't remain silent. I don't talk about Jesus just to convert my son. I talk about Jesus because I can't not talk about Jesus. I can't not talk about the amazing way God has kept his promise to send us a savior. I can't not talk about how Jesus fulfills every requirement of the law and allows us to live freely, not tripping over each rule and regulation but to be led by his spirit into a life of liberty. I know you think Mom and I are just talking, but this faith I've found, the faith that has so generously found me, is real, honey. I'm compelled to try to live like Jesus, and that means I need to be more caring and loving and sharing and helpful. That's who I am, and that's how I live. It's not a show. It's not just to convert my son, although I do want him to know all about Jesus so he can love him and accept his amazing sacrificial gift too—yes, I want that. But I can't help myself. I've got to do what I do because of who has touched me and changed my life. I pray you too will one day understand why I do what I do.

Exemplary Faith Encourages Others

Eunice's and Lois's faith is encouraging, in such a way that Paul uses their names to encourage Timothy to keep spreading the Word of God. What powerful influence these women must have had if just the mention of their names by Paul encouraged Timothy. Just thinking of the exemplary life these women had lived renewed and revived their son and grandson. Timothy apparently didn't just remember his grandmother's great cooking and his mother's patiently helping him with his homework. These women contributed much more than a good meal and help with academics; they shared their lifesaving and life-giving faith with the young man in their charge.

They probably had no idea that Timothy would grow up to be a valuable assistant to Paul, arguably the biggest influence on the Christian faith today. Yet they instilled their faith through living as examples for the impressionable Timothy, who was gifted in sharing the gospel message with others. They had a hand in Timothy's gift being nurtured and developed. They planted the seed that would go on to grow and blossom as he worked closely with Paul (2 Timothy 1:6). Mama and Grandma just by being their faith-filled selves made a major impact on Timothy and in turn our faith.

Sometimes in our modern world where women are heads of companies and countries, prominent attorneys and doctors, policy makers and shot callers, if you do not hold such an esteemed position, you may be left wondering if you can make a difference. If your platform is not large—perhaps you do not hold a big title or travel the world sharing the truth of Christ—you may wonder if your small efforts can make a difference in such a large world. Maybe you don't teach or sing or put on big workshops for others to be lifted up and encouraged in the faith, but Lois and Eunice can remind you that influence may begin small, but you have no idea how far its reach can flow. Regardless of your status in life, your socioeconomic position, or your title, you can influence others and make an impact larger than you can begin to imagine.

You don't have to be well known to show someone right next to you how to live in faith. You don't have to be the person in front of a camera or microphone to show your household how to trust and believe in God. No, your children, your friends, your coworkers can all get a front-row glimpse of activated faith by seeing how you live each day. In fact, only those closest to you can observe your faith in handling life every day.

How do you face trials? How do you deal with the ups and downs of life? How do you thrive during a routine, mundane season in life? Is your faith intact? Do you wake up praising God or complaining about the day? Do you thank God when you arrive home safely, or do you moan more about the traffic jam? Do your children or those who live with you or around you hear you thanking God for your job and the ability to use your gifts and skills, or do they hear more about your annoying coworkers and boss? Do you end the day thanking God and counting your blessings, or do you finish it off with yet another complaint on your lips? How do you, the up-close-and-personal example of faith, treat those in your household? Your true colors can sometimes only be seen by those closest to you. What are they seeing? Is it faith that can encourage them to keep pressing and seeking God? Is it the type of faith such that at just the mention of your name they can be encouraged to keep going and to use their gifts for God's people?

Just as I was writing about Lois and her daughter Eunice, a friend called me to report on her mother's health. A band of us had been praying specifically for more than a week about my friend's mom's health. When you're eighty-six and your heart malfunctions and you are hospitalized, it is a scary situation for you and your family. My friend lives on the opposite coast from her mother, so she was particularly concerned, as she was unable to be by her side.

But on this day, I was happy to hear my friend's report that the doctors had found the problem and thought it was relatively easy to fix, and they assessed her mother and thought she was healthy enough to withstand the procedure and recover well. I breathed a sigh of relief and whispered a prayer of gratitude to God. However, my praise soon turned to good old-fashioned laughter as my friend continued to share golden words of wisdom, as she often does, from the lips of her mother. While my girlfriend and her brother and sister were fretting, conferencing with the doctors, searching the Internet for similar cases, texting us to pray, her mom was not worried. While she was uncomfortable and in some pain, this woman of faith was still her funny, quick-witted self. "I don't know why y'all are so worried, over here asking the doctors all of these questions and calling me all of the time. Don't y'all know I serve a God who is a healer, and if it is my time to go, I will go happily to meet my God? But if it's not, I'll be right here. Don't you know I've had this procedure before and things went very well? So why all of the fussing?"

Naturally as a concerned adult child, my friend reminded her mother that she had been much younger the last time she had this procedure—a mere sixty-nine years old.

"God was God when I was sixty-nine, and God is still God now that I'm eighty-six. What's the issue, dear?"

What faith! What truth! What lovely wisdom this seasoned woman of God poured out to my friend and her siblings, who in turn shared with other friends and reminded us all to hang tight to the faith we proclaim. God is God, yesterday, today, and tomorrow, and that's good, liberating news that can sustain you during the darkest, most trying times of life.

When I think of the witness of older women like my friend's mother and Timothy's grandmother Lois, I'm also reminded that we don't have to be young and full of boundless energy to make an impact. Grandmothers and elderly people have lots of value and wisdom to pass on. Life doesn't stop when you turn a certain age. In fact, it can actually begin—especially when you consider what you've learned and all you've survived. Grandmothers have lots to share. Grandmothers have a faith sometimes rooted in years of trusting and depending on God. Grandmothers have stories to tell, and if they are willing to be vulnerable and open up, they can make a difference in their grandchildren's and in other people's lives.

Grandmothers can also give a glimpse of faith in action to the people they touch each day. If they have embraced their stage in life, relinquished the temptation to live on the corner of regret and bitterness, their faith can shine through their lives and they can leave endearing impressions on their grandkids and those around them. In some families, grandmothers carry the faith; they are often the first ones to introduce younger ones to Christ. Grandmothers are valuable sources for the young and the old, and with proper perspective they can embrace their role and stage in life.

Self-Check

As a woman of faith seeking to influence others, is prayer your default method, or is complaining to your girl pal on the phone the first thing you do? Is your conversation riddled with "I know God will make a way" or "I don't know how in the world this will work"? Is your attitude hopeful, reflecting the faith you have in God to make all things beautiful in time, or do you flat-out see the ugly around us and call it out as such and expect nothing more?

Oh, what joy it is to live next to people of faith, people of hope, people of expectation. You can sense the atmosphere change when these types of women walk into the room—people are not running away from them but are running toward them. People may not even know why they are attracted to women of faith, but it's the hope they bring, the confidence they hold, and the light they shine. Calling their names can summon a smile. Thinking about their lives can give you encouragement to keep going. Seeing their joy can remind you to keep your head up even in the midst of trials and tribulations. Hearing their testimonies reminds you that there is a God. Their lives point back to God and God's goodness. I want to be that type of woman of faith.

In this dark world, we need more faith heroes, those who tell us about and show us the love of God. Those who remind us to hope and wait and trust in God. Those who point to how big God is rather than how big the issue is. These are the women I want to be around. This is the type of woman I want to be remembered as. It can be tough, especially if we live in the natural state. You can always find someone who will want to complain. You can always find someone who will want to rehash a situation and gossip about another woman. But if we resist these temptations, they will flee (James 4:7). If we commit to live by the spirit—seeking to walk and talk with God—we will see hope and joy and peace. We will be encouragers rather than complainers. We will depend on God rather than on others to bring joy and peace.

I want to deposit hope and joy in the people I touch—whether my family, friends, neighbors, or strangers. I want them to remember that I trusted in God, that I believed in God, that I waited for God to make a change. I don't want them to remember the pity parties I had and the bad news I was prompt to deliver. I want them to know more than that. I want them to remember more than that. I want to be life giving, not life robbing. I want to be like Lois and Eunice.

When Paul says those women had strong faith, he tells us that their lives were filled with faith—from the rising to the setting of the sun. They didn't live in contradiction to what they believed. Can people say the same about you? Do your friends from work call you faith-filled? Do the women on the committee at the school know you're a Christian, not because of the cross around your neck but because of your actions—your temperament, how you handle conflict and disappointment and the issues of life?

I bet Lois and Eunice were known throughout the community as faith-filled—particularly because Paul called them out. I bet they were known as prayer warriors by their community. They were trusted and dependable people because of the lives they lived and how they poured selflessly into other people.

When I was in my mid-thirties and had not been married or borne a child, I was talking to another single and childless friend the day before Mother's Day. She asked if I felt sad around this time because I didn't have children. When I thought about her question, I said quickly and certainly, "No." I dug deeper and asked myself why didn't I feel empty without a child. Hadn't I always just assumed I'd get married and have children, along with all the other things I had dreamed about in life? But in my mid-thirties with no prospect of a husband nor any plans to adopt or become a single mama, I was faced with the very real possibility of not having a biological child. But I didn't feel empty. I didn't even feel alone. I felt like I had planted seeds in the lives of others. I had served as an active mentor in several young women's lives. I had taught teens in Sunday school and often heard from some students. I had taken care of other kids—and I felt full. I felt like I had been a parent, minus the full-time responsibility.

While I do have a biological child of my own now, I am happy that I was full and fruitful before she even came along. I'm happy that I found fulfillment in giving and planting and helping others. I'm happy that I can say my life has not been in vain; my life has not just been about me and my goals and my acquisitions. My life has been impactful to others, and I pray my life can continue to influence others to see God. I pray my trials can show others that I depend on God, and God has an amazing way of pulling me through at just the right time. I pray that others will see me as Paul and Timothy saw Eunice and Lois: not just as a mama and a grandmother but as a woman of faith—a woman of strong, certain faith in God.

⌢

I am Eunice. I am Lois. I live for more than myself. I live to show others the way to Christ. I live so my life shows others that I trust in God. I live so others will see that I believe in God, that I believe in someone much bigger than myself. I lean and depend on the certainty of God in a life filled with uncertainty. Even if my household doesn't believe, I believe and my faith shines through regardless of my circumstances. My children know of my faith, my neighbors know of my faith, my coworkers know of my faith—not because of what I say, but because of the way I live. When I am remembered, I will be remembered as a woman of faith.

Mary Magdalene

Successful women live redeemed lives—
because of and in spite of our past.

After Jesus rose from the dead early on Sunday
morning, the first person who saw him was Mary
Magdalene, the woman from whom he had cast out
seven demons.

(Mark 16:9, NLT)

After this, while Jesus was traveling through some
cities and small towns, he preached and told the Good
News about God's kingdom. The twelve apostles were
with him, and also some women who had been healed
of sicknesses and evil spirits: Mary, called Magdalene,
from whom seven demons had gone out; Joanna, the
wife of Cuza (the manager of Herod's house); Susanna;
and many others. These women used their own money
to help Jesus and his apostles.

(Luke 8:1–3, NCV)

As women and as humans, there's no escaping the labels that can so easily attach themselves to us, leading people to mistakenly use our label as our name and confuse our identity with what has been said about us. Labels can make people see us for what we've done rather than for who we truly are. Some labels are slapped on us at birth: cute, chubby, sweet, colicky, cranky, good. Some labels were acquired while we grew up: skinny, bony, mean, smart, talented, precocious, sassy, brazen, strong willed. Others are whispered behind our backs as we get older: killjoy, negative, man-hater, loose, unavailable, cold, charming, Christian, hard worker, dependable, flaky, late, optimistic—the list can go on and on. And even still there are labels we place on ourselves, a composite of what we've heard, what we've experienced, what we see in the mirror, and what we feel inside: ugly, big nose, big hips, big butt, small breasts, big gut, undesirable, insecure, lost, unloved.

If we could first release ourselves from the labels and begin to see ourselves as God does (see Psalm 139), we'd live much happier and more content lives. And then if others could see past what they've heard of us—or even what they've known us to do—we could experience new depth in relationships and live past our labels. But that sounds like another story and a lifelong goal for each of us.

Still, there is a successful woman in the Bible who lived with a label for her entire life, and she shows us how to live in a redeemed state even when others only see your past. She is named Mary Magdalene. She is labeled as the "woman from whom [Jesus] cast out seven demons." She is lauded throughout the gospel as a faithful follower of Jesus, yet whenever her contributions to Jesus' ministry are mentioned, so is her label. Even in the historic and profound moment when she witnesses the resurrection of our savior, the promised victory at the crux of the Christian faith, she is described as the one from whom Jesus cast out seven demons. The gospel writer is retelling the pivotal story of our faith—the Lord has risen—and he includes Mary's label. The label follows Mary everywhere she goes, and this is no lamb in a nursery rhyme. This label is attached to her name like a bad habit or a pesky gnat. She can't escape it. Everyone who knew Mary must have known her by the label: Jesus cast out seven demons from that woman.

A Dark Past

What kind of life had Mary lived with seven demons raging inside of her? Could her malady have been schizophrenia? Bipolar disorder? Depression? With seven, it could have been all of them and then some. What antics had she performed, not being in her right mind or even being able to control her faculties at all times? Who had she gone off on? Who had she dissed? Had she killed anyone? Taken someone's man? Hurt someone's child? How had she coped with seven demons? What ways had she tried to self-medicate to stop the raging war inside of her? How had she looked? Where had she lived? What places had she been kicked out of? Where was her family? Had they given up on this woman who always showed up with seven other personalities? Who knows, but apparently those seven demons were known just as much as Mary. And as much as she was known for those seven demons, I think people had no real clue what was happening inside of her, being split between joy, happiness, rage, sadness, insecurity, fear, anxiety, and so on. We knew she had seven demons, but how did she really feel? I hear her sharing just a bit.

Yeah, I'm that girl. I'm the one. I'm the one who used to have seven demons raging inside of me, each one fighting for attention, fighting to be heard and seen. Yes, I was a mess. I didn't know which way I was going. I often didn't know where I was or who I was. All I know is I wanted the war inside of my mind to stop. I wanted to stop hearing voices and to stop talking back. I wanted to just once be able to walk into a room and feel okay, to not see and feel the stares followed by whispers inside and outside my head. I wanted to have one night of restful sleep, not tormented by the voices that got louder and louder as I sat more still. I wanted to be able to walk without looking over my shoulder because two of my voices constantly reminded me that someone, something, was out to get me. That's all I ever wanted. I tried to self-medicate, but nothing worked for more than a few moments.

Then one day, someone mentioned a man who was healing people. He wasn't charging them or asking for favors in return. I've had a few of those types of "healers" come into my life. No, this man, they said, was different and powerful and compassionate and sure of himself. I heard about him, and I just had to see him for myself. I was afraid. My voices told me not to go to the meeting. But somehow, some way, I pressed my way through. I made it to the man named Jesus, and he healed me. He looked into my eyes and called me daughter and told me I was healed. He said a word and the demons fled.

At that very moment, I knew I needed to follow this man, learn what he was teaching, and commit my life to serving him. Nothing had ever worked, but now I was a member of his family, even though my own family had disowned me and distanced themselves from me a long time ago. This wonderful man said he came to give me a good and full life. He said if I followed his teachings, I could have peace. I could have rest. That's all I ever wanted.

Mary had lived most of her life with these demons, but even after she was healed, she was known by her past. When someone saw her, they always recalled her antics before she met Christ. When people saw her, they immediately thought about the demons that had controlled her life for so long. How does it feel to walk through life being known for who you were or what you did or your condition? How does it feel to be known not by your name but by what happened to you? Victim, failure, divorcée, the woman who...

It can be demeaning and demoralizing to hear whispers about your past every time you walk into a room. It can hurt to run into people and all they have to say is, "I remember when you were…I remember when you did that." People seem to get joy out of sharing the good old times when it is at someone else's expense. But I don't hear Mary Magdalene complaining about the whispers and the stigma placed upon her like an old sticker unable to be removed—even with the toughest cleaners. No, every time I see her in scripture, I see her attached to Jesus. She knows how to live with a stigma, walking closely with the one who removed her shame and redeemed her life.

Stick Close to Jesus

Mary didn't seem fazed by the name-calling or reminders of her past because she was too focused on her redeemer. Look at each instance she's mentioned in scripture. In Luke 8:2, Mary, from whom Jesus delivered seven demons, is listed with the twelve disciples who traveled with our savior from town to town sharing the life-changing news of his God-sent mission. She, like the twelve disciples, stayed close to Jesus, soaking up all of his astounding teaching and witnessing the miracles he performed. She hung out with Jesus, her mind focused and fixed on him, to keep her in peace despite what others said about her past. When we are close to Jesus, we recall his miracles and even see them in everyday life. We replay his teachings, which are able to keep us in perfect peace no matter what others may be saying about us. Mary was fixated and focused, unable to be deterred by her past.

In the same passage in Luke, it is also notable that Mary, Joanna, and Susanna's names are listed with the twelve disciples. These women had to have been faithful followers, like the twelve "official" disciples. They not only followed Jesus, but scripture records that they also supported his ministry "out of their own means." They believed so much in Jesus and what he was doing that they dug deep into their own pockets and supported him. Mary and these women showed their gratitude for Jesus through their own benevolence.

When we see Mary again in Mark 15:40–41 and Matthew 27:55–56, she's right there with Mary, the mother of James and Joses (another label follows that Mary), and Salome. These women were witnesses to the crucifixion of their Lord. The women who had supported Jesus during his life were also witnesses of his death. As heartrending as it must have been, these faithful women watched as Jesus was tortured and put to death. Their devotion also led them to watch Jesus' burial (Matthew 27:57–61). They couldn't believe what was happening and they couldn't desert their Lord, not even as he was put into his grave. True devotion shows up, even—or especially— when it is heart-wrenching, difficult, and tragic.

I also see Mary at the resurrection, the glorious moment

each Christian rejoices in. Mary, who was weeping at the tomb, is honored by Jesus. He honors her devotion; he honors her commitment to press through even with her label by revealing himself to her first and telling her that he has risen (John 20:14–17). He has done exactly what he said he would do and has defeated death to give every believer a new life, hope, and power. He honored and further redeemed this woman's life. Jesus gave her the honor of being the first one to tell the good news: He has risen.

The woman who once had seven demons can now proclaim, based on what she alone has seen, that the Lord is not dead; he is alive. Her past may be a part of her story, but it is not all of her story. She has a new chapter to add, a better chapter, a chapter filled with redemption for all. Her story is much bigger than her seven demons; her label may be present, but it can't overshadow the resurrection story she gets to experience and to share.

So Mary's label didn't stop her devotion. In fact, it fueled her service to Jesus. She stayed close to Jesus during his life, his death, and ultimately his resurrection. She took care of his needs and made sure he was comfortable. She mourned when he died and rejoiced when he rose. Her devotion had to be her way of saying thank you to Jesus and acknowledging what he had done.

How do you thank God for saving you? How do you thank Jesus for turning you around and setting you on a new path? In what ways do you acknowledge God for renaming you and renewing you and reviving you? Does your service and devotion to God reflect all he has done for you? Do you use your own resources to help those suffering from the conditions from which you have been delivered? Are you helping to spread the gospel message of redemption and restoration?

Labels Can Be Good Reminders

Like Mary, the one from whom Jesus cast out seven demons, when we realize just what we've overcome, how God has brought us through, how Jesus has fixed our conditions and transformed our lives, we're undeterred by the whispers or labels or names we're called. In fact, these taunts or descriptors may serve as much-needed reminders. I could have been down today, but I heard your whisper. I heard you say, "That's the one who had seven demons," and all of a sudden I was reminded of whence I came, just how far God has brought me, and I had to stop and thank God right then and there. Your whispering caused me to remember what I had been through. "That's the one who used to date…" Oh, thank you, I forgot how God got me out of that situation. "That's the one who was sick with…" "That's the one who came from…" "She's the one who got put out, or lost her job, or did…" Yes, that's me, and thank you for the reminder!

Sometimes when we start anew—move to a better home, a different neighborhood, or even out of town—we can leave behind what we used to be. We leave behind the name-calling, we leave behind the naughty acts, we move into a new place and enter a new phase, and we can "forget" about what we did. But forgetting is not always good. It can make us immune to the hurts of those going through what we've been through. If no one is reminding us about the seven demons buried in our closets never to be resurrected again, perhaps we can get a bit too pious and forget that we even had seven demons. We can look at the sister acting like we used to and shake our heads because we've forgotten just how far we have come. We can join in whispers about others' sins, forgetting what we used to do and how we used to do it—and enjoy it.

As annoying as a label can be, sometimes it's good to be reminded where we came from. When I hear about my demons, I can reach out to a sister going through the same thing and remind her that there is hope. I can donate money to the cure, like Mary and the other women. I can visit shelters and share my story and resources with the sisters there. I can even visit prisons, not to give pity offerings, but to give hope offerings. I know I look cleaned up now, but you just don't know. I've seen some things and I've seen some places. And what Jesus has done is written all over my story.

When you share your personal and intimate testimony, you're not sharing what God *can do*; you are sharing what God *has done* in your life. You become a walking billboard, promoting the transforming power of God, showcasing God's unconditional love, which is available to all who only believe. Your story is powerful. Your story can point the way for someone who is lost.

When I was asked to speak at a women's conference where the theme was "Real Women with Real Issues," I prayed about a particular subject. When I felt prompted to speak out about depression, I was scared. I had served at this very same church while in seminary about nine years ago. I had poured my heart into the youth, trying to help them understand the biblical platitudes and excitement for Jesus that adults often exhibited yet left many youth wondering what the big deal was. At that church, I think I was seen as the exuberant youth minister who was committed to helping youth find their way. I was not known as the woman who fought to get out of bed—and didn't sometimes—nor as the one who had been to therapy and even taken medicine for a period of time for a depressive state she couldn't shake for several years, even with continuous prayers. But I still felt like I needed to have an honest talk with these women and share that even women who have faith suffer from depression. I needed to share my journey and come out of the closet and let the women know my story, even as I was living it out.

When I posted on Facebook about my subject and to invite others to the conference, I received countless messages in my inbox. Women and men were suffering silently; some were friends I actually communicated with on a regular basis, yet I didn't know of their conditions.

Just my post about what I had been through and still went through was encouraging to others and had touched them enough for them to let me know what they too had been going through.

I started blogging about depression and faith and received even more messages. People needed to hear this story. People needed me to open up and share what I had been through. Our stories are like that. They are intimate, up-close-and-personal descriptions of what God has carried us through. When we focus on the healer more than our problem or our shame, we can tell our story. We can share boldly how God has gotten or is getting us through and transforming our lives. We are the billboards for God. We are the advertisers for all God has done and can do for others. And when our gratefulness to God overpowers our shame and fear, we can speak out and show Christ to others.

Who needs to hear your story today? Who needs to know what God has done for you? Who needs to know the awfulness Jesus has delivered you from? Is it you who needs a reminder? Or is it someone else? Your label may remind someone else or yourself just how awesome our God is. People don't know your full story until you share it with them; rumors don't tell the entire truth, and labels can be deceiving. But when you share what Jesus has done, lives can be changed. When you recall how you used to do one thing and now you do something differently, others can be encouraged to follow your Christ too. Labels don't have to be all bad; sure, they cloud others' vision, but they also remind us of how far we've come, and they can give us a chance to point to our healer and changer. Let the labels of your past point to your redeemer.

—

I am Mary Magdalene and I am more than my label. I am not my past. I am new. I am redeemed. I will not forget my past because it reminds me just how far God has brought me. I thank you, Lord, for casting out my demons and giving me a new life. Remind me to always give you the praise and honor and glory for the things you have done in my life. You are worthy to be praised. I am who I am because of all you've done! I have nothing to be ashamed of, but so much to praise you for. Because of your touch, I am new. I am redeemed.

Priscilla

Successful women can be secure partners with men.

Give my greetings to Priscilla and Aquila, who work together with me in Christ Jesus.

(Romans 16:3, NCV)

Apollos began to speak very boldly in the synagogue, and when Priscilla and Aquila heard him, they took him to their home and helped him better understand the way of God.

(Acts 18:26, NCV)

Successful women can also have successful marriages, sharing with their husbands as partners in life. One such woman in the Bible is Priscilla. She is married to Aquila, and every time we see this power couple in scripture, they are together, working side by side to tell others about Christ: "Give my greetings to Priscilla and Aquila"

(Romans 16:3); Paul was "accompanied by Priscilla and Aquila" (Acts 18:18); "Priscilla and Aquila greet you in the Lord" (1 Corinthians 16:19).

This dynamic duo are coworkers with Paul. They share the good news, the lifesaving and life-changing gospel of Christ's life, death, and resurrection, with others, together. One is not ahead of the other. One is not listed as the chief and the other the co-chief. One is not listed as the pilot and the other as the copilot. They were thought of as one, equal partners. Together, they made each other better and spread the gospel of Christ.

Notably, when mentioned in scripture, Priscilla is most often listed before her husband, which was not congruent with the patriarchy of the time. While we don't see signs of Priscilla being more dominant than her husband, she was clearly not looked upon as less than her husband. She was at the very least considered equally as wise and loving and smart and prolific and devoted as her husband, or any other man for that matter. Why else would she be listed first so often when referring to the duo, even by Paul, who has written some controversial words about women?

Collaborators, Not Competitors

Even still, with Priscilla most often mentioned first, there's not a hint of competition with these two. They focused on the mission of sharing Christ, and they did it with apparent wisdom and grace. Dear Priscilla, there are some twenty-first-century women who need to know your secret to living in harmony with your lifelong mate, even as you work so closely together. Can you share?

Well, first and foremost, my sisters, I came to know Jesus through the teachings of Paul. I listened to his testimony. I heard how his life was changed, and I made the choice to learn more about Jesus for myself. I listened to all that was written about him. I listened to those who had lived during the time he walked the earth. I became a Bible student myself, taking in all I could about this man named Jesus and the new way of life he instituted for people who believed. I had my own relationship with Jesus first. I realized that knowing Jesus made me secure, regardless of what else was going on in my life, regardless of my husband, regardless of my job, regardless of my looks. Regardless, Jesus made me secure. My title as a wife didn't do it for me; only my relationship with Christ gave me security.

Once I heard about Jesus, my whole outlook on life and on myself changed. I heard about how he helped the woman at the well, and I knew Jesus didn't dislike women like our society did. I knew Jesus actually spoke to women and treated them as human beings. While I grew up in a home that didn't value women, I learned to value myself, all because of what Jesus said and did to the women he met.

I even heard how he helped that woman who had seven demons—What's her name? Mary Magdalene. She had been certifiable before her change, but then after the change, this woman was a completely new person. I knew if Jesus could change her, he was for real. He had some real power. And she was so sweet, you couldn't detect a hint of demon in her, but people never let you forget how she used to be. The one who was wild and crazy and who everyone tried to avoid in the streets was now helping Jesus and his mission. It was something to hear about.

Hearing personal stories made me believe in Jesus. And when I believed, I became a better woman. I desired to live according to Jesus' teaching—loving and forgiving, serving others with joy, including my husband. When Aquila started grasping all that I had learned, he too became secure in Christ. We'd spend lots of time just marveling over this Jesus and sharing our thoughts on all he had done and all that was being said about him. Our faith grew together. Our love of Christ grew more and more each day as we learned more and shared more. It was amazing. It was powerful how our love for Christ transformed us individually as well as how it transformed our relationship. We began to share more with each other, not worrying about ourselves as much. As we poured into each other's lives, forgetting about ourselves, we realized that we were better. We were actually being taken care of by the other person. Aquila wanted to make me happy and comfortable, and I wanted to make him happy and comfortable. And we both did that for each other.

After believing in Jesus and studying his teachings, I found that I became more patient with Aquila. I stopped talking negatively about my husband and I started seeing all that God was doing in his life and through his life. That had to be God moving in me. Aquila wasn't always perfect, but neither was I. However, with Christ as our focus, we desired to forgive each other more quickly. We prayed for help, and we got it.

When Aquila and I realized how much we had changed because of our belief in Christ, we decided we needed to do more for this movement. We needed to share more about Jesus and his love and grace and mercy. We talked to Paul and told him we wanted to help. He was glad. He needed the help and he said he trusted us.

Paul said he had observed how well we worked together and how we embodied the unity of Christ, that when we worked together it wasn't as male or female, but as one (Galatians 3:28). We are one in Christ. The Lord didn't see me as a mere woman, the weaker sex, the one with the emotions and a big mouth. He saw me as he formed me, and I was happy about that.

My husband also saw me as his partner. When you have someone in your corner, and you know he's in your corner, you don't have to fight for a position. I served him, and he served me. We flowed like that. We were just so happy to be serving Jesus and helping Paul spread the word; it was our life's calling. I guess when you do what makes you happy and what you know you're supposed to be doing, you don't have to jockey for position either. Every morning when I woke up, I knew what I was doing and why I was doing it. The added bonus was that I got to do it with my husband too. I was a lucky girl.

Oh, sure, Aquila and I had disagreements. We were still humans, but we handled those disagreements differently as our relationship with Christ grew. We talked to each other, not at each other. We listened to each other, and our defenses were not automatically up. Because I knew Aquila wanted to be like Christ, I could trust him, and because he knew I wanted to imitate Christ, he could trust me. This made our communication more open and free. We said what we felt in love and gently. We prayed about everything—especially the issues we disagreed on—and we found solutions when we listened to God's spirit that guided us.

We even changed how we treated others we disagreed with; we didn't argue with them anymore or embarrass them in public. One time, a man named Apollos was teaching in the synagogue (Acts 18:24–28). Some of the stuff he was saying was not quite right, but we could tell that he had a good heart and was passionate about sharing the gospel. Some might have stood up and stopped him right there. You know, showed him up and told him to get it right. But no, that's not how Aquila and I thought it should be handled. We were sensitive to the situation and we wanted to show love, not hostility, to our brother.

So you know what we did? We called Apollos over and had dinner with him. There's something equalizing and inviting about eating together. We got to know him better as we shared a meal. We opened our home to him and let him know we cared about him. Then we shared our thoughts on baptism and Christ, and he got it. He received it well. We were pleased because we wanted him to continue doing his work, but we wanted him to correct his mistake too. He went on to preach Christ to many others. Because we helped Apollos better understand, I'm sure many more people came to Christ after hearing Apollos's words.

You know that when you are joyous inside, filled with the love of Christ, the way you deal with others will be affected— particularly the way you correct others. We didn't need to embarrass Apollos or call him out. We were gentle and prayer- ful and genuine. I guess our concern came through. We treat each other the very same way. I know Aquila's heart. I know he loves God and he loves me, so when I have an issue with him, I go to him genuinely seeking to resolve the issue. I don't attack my husband; that doesn't make things better. I gently and in love share with him what's on my mind. And he hears me. We talk and we work to resolve the issue. It's a beautiful partnership, and because we love Christ, our relationship is so much better and so different than it was before.

Priscilla can definitely show successful women today how our relationship with Christ affects the rest of our relationships with our spouses, friends, children, cowork- ers, parents, teachers, and so on. You can't have a genuine relationship with Christ and not have that relationship influence all of your other relationships. Yes, we're all growing as followers of Christ, and we have more to attain and understand, but when the love of Christ takes hold of our lives, this love begins to spread like a wildfire, and others can feel the impact and change.

We don't always understand our transformation ourselves. Forgiveness, while hard, is now a priority. We don't sleep well until we can talk it over with the person we have offended or who has offended us. We pray constantly about the situation until it is released. We help those we may have cursed before our change; we seek harmony and peace over strife and contention. We're not the same.

And when contention arises, we handle it differently. We find ourselves apologizing more, not because we do more wrong, but because we're acutely aware of how we can offend and we want to correct the issue. Humility takes hold of us when we consider Christ's humble example. We don't always need the last word; it's just not helpful and it doesn't always advance love. We seek to release bitterness, fighting to let go of whatever grasps us—for ourselves, for our partners, for peace.

When you know the peace of Christ, you crave it. You desire it when you don't feel at peace, and you'll do whatever it takes to get back to that harmonious place. Even when you feel old feelings of jealousy and competitiveness creeping up inside of you (as they will), your connection to God's spirit reminds you that those feelings are not like Christ. Or whenever you have a gossip session about someone, you feel convicted. You feel as if you've grieved the spirit of Christ inside of you (Ephesians 4:30)—and you have. You repent quickly and seek help for your issues. You desire to let your old habits go, you pray to let them go, and eventually they are released. Why? Because you are different. You are a confident and secure woman of God, and you don't want anything to break that blessed flow.

Priscilla's life is an example of a woman remembered for her work in sharing Christ with others and doing this work in harmony with her husband. In modern society, where divorces seem commonplace, her example reminds us that it is possible for a woman and a man to live in harmony and build a legacy together, especially if they allow the love of Christ to reign first in their lives and then let this love from Christ permeate their relationship. And while I can't begin to provide marital advice in one chapter in a book about successful women, I can share a few insights I've garnered from observing successful marriages, like that of my parents, who were married almost forty-four years before my mom died, and even my own, which while still very much a work in progress has shown me more about myself than I could have ever imagined and made me appreciate even more God's unconditional love for me.

Marriage is a reflection of Christ's love for the church. In fact, several places in the Bible refer to Christians as the bride and Christ as the bridegroom. Christ loves us unconditionally, with our attitudes and all of our issues. It's a pure love based on God's commitment to those who believe, not on what we do. And while this analogy in no way excuses abusive and unhealthy behavior, I do think it reminds us to overlook our partner's imperfections, idiosyncrasies, and annoying habits. Instead, we strive to live as a unit and a reflection of God's love.

Rather than focusing on what he is or is not doing, we can see our partners through the love we have committed to share. When I wake up each morning committed to love my husband, I am committed to serving him—in whatever way may be of help to him. I often have to check my attitude and pray to remind myself to consider him, to consider what makes him happy and not just what will make me happy.

I admit that as a single woman, and even now as a married woman, I struggled hard with the dreaded *s* words—*submission* and *service*. I was an independent, strong-willed, goal-oriented woman. I am also the youngest of my siblings, so after years of being bossed around, now as a grown woman I really don't want anyone telling me what to do. (Funny, I see this attitude even in my six-year-old only child, so it may be more than a youngest-child syndrome.) This attitude is a part of who I am, and I can own that now (which took some tough introspective studying).

When I really started to believe that Christ loves me and I should submit to that love and authority, I then realized that if my husband loves God and is committed to following him, then maybe—just maybe—I could submit to him and we could submit to each other (Ephesians 5:21). By learning to submit to God's will for my life, I also learned how to listen more to my husband without the fear of being told what to do or bossed around. I heard him out; he often had a different opinion or viewpoint. Slowly, I learned that when it came to issues in our marriage, he was not out to hurt me. He was looking out for my best interests, and I could yield to him. In turn, he's come back to me and yielded on some issues too. We prompt each other to rethink some things, which allows us both to be shaped into better people. My marriage got better when I started to rely on Derrick more. I had to work through my strong-woman issues and learn to trust him, and one thing that helped me trust him was seeing that he really did care and love me and want the very best for me, even if that looked different than I thought it should.

A pivotal moment for me occurred when we had a fire scare in our condo building one lazy Saturday morning. A loud knock on our front door forced both of us to run to see what the matter was. A neighbor said everyone was leaving the building while a fireman stood behind her with a bewildered look on his face. I got my jacket and quickly exited our home, expecting Derrick to follow behind me. He hesitated. He said perhaps we needed to stay out of the way and wait for instructions from the fire department, especially since the fireman hadn't told us to evacuate. Still, I set out for the stairway. I didn't listen for instructions; I did what I thought was right. And Derrick reluctantly followed. As we entered the stairway, smoke filled the air. Derrick murmured, "This isn't right. We shouldn't be in the stairway. We're walking into smoke, and we don't know where it is coming from." I didn't understand him. I didn't stop to try to figure it out. I just wanted to find the exit, so I cautiously stepped through a cloud of smoke in a dark stairwell, gripped the railing, and made my way down four flights of stairs.

It turns out the fire was on the first floor of the building, on the opposite side from our apartment on the fourth floor. Since the fire department had already gotten it under control, they didn't think residents should come down toward the fire, but too many of us had already started to panic and self-evacuate, so they let us come down. Derrick was right. He had thought about the situation and realized the stairways could be the worst place for us to be if the fire was not on our side of the building or if the firemen were trying to get upstairs. His concern was evident. His desire to protect me and us was clear.

As I reflected on that harried Saturday morning, I fully understood that I had truly married a protector. My husband desired to keep me safe. When I put down my defenses, looking for the abuse and mistreatment, I saw the love. Even when his opinion is different than mine, I can be confident that he wants to protect me; he wants what is best for me. So now, when we have a difference of opinion, I try to stop and listen a little more carefully. I can't always see what he sees from my vantage point, so listening is critical.

Submission is easier when you believe you both have each other's back. Service is done out of your desire to care for each other. I embraced the opportunity to work with my partner and produce a healthy and happy marriage, and I still have to recommit to this desire each and every day. It's not the easiest thing I've ever done—it's far from it, but working in relationship with my partner has brought me joy.

And there's joy to be found in relationship with others. If we believe in harmonious unions and submit ourselves to Christ and allow our relationship with Christ to impact our connections, we can find harmony and peace and love too—with our spouse, our friends, our coworkers, or our children. Priscilla proves it.

—

I am Priscilla. I know my worth and I know my value. It's not because of my size, my shape, my skin, my degree, my heritage, or my hair. It's because I am a child of God. It's because of who Christ has made me to be. I have love. I know love. I am loved, and I want to share the love of Christ wherever I go. I long for others to be truly connected to Christ so they can experience the peace and joy I know. I am humble because of all Christ has done for me. I am patient because Christ has been patient with me. I have self-control because God's spirit gives it to me. I have joy, love, and peace because I am connected to Christ. I abide in him, and he abides in me. My life is different. My life is complete. My life is whole. I am a successful woman.

Lydia

Successful women can handle their business.

On the Sabbath day we went outside the city gate to the river where we thought we would find a special place for prayer. Some women had gathered there, so we sat down and talked with them. One of the listeners was a woman named Lydia from the city of Thyatira whose job was selling purple cloth. She worshiped God, and he opened her mind to pay attention to what Paul was saying. She and all the people in her house were baptized. Then she invited us to her home, saying, "If you think I am truly a believer in the Lord, then come stay in my house." And she persuaded us to stay with her.

(Acts 16:13–15, NCV)

Women have influence. Successful women have lots of influence. Successful women of faith hold influence that can shape the world and change lives. That's serious and important influence.

Look at successful woman of the Bible Lydia for just a glimpse at the power women hold. Lydia was from Thyatira and is written about as Luke, the writer of Acts, chronicles the early ministry of Paul, the apostle who is most responsible for spreading the news of the gospel. Luke was a companion of Paul, and he wrote about what happened so others might believe and receive the grace, unconditional love, and salvation Christ offered.

Luke says that Paul and his group had been trying to go to several different places but were blocked by the spirit (Acts 16:6–10)—because sometimes we're just not supposed to be where we want to be; our mission is to be elsewhere at a particular time. If we're smart, we'll thank God for roadblocks and detours instead of forcing our way through and making things happen. If we're smart, we'll say, "Oh well, I guess I wasn't supposed to do that today," and keep it moving. Paul did. And he and his group ended up near Thyatira, where Lydia, our successful woman, lived.

While Paul was trying to go in another direction, a group of faithful women had been meeting in Thyatira. These women worshiped God but had not received the good news of Christ. They met faithfully to share scripture and pray. There was no synagogue for them to gather in Thyatira at the time, but that didn't stop them. These women met by a river. They didn't let not having a building stop them from gathering.

Sometimes the best work can be done outside the walls of an institution. Sometimes the most sincere prayers can be sent up outside of human-built walls. Praying by the riverside connects us even more to the creator of water and land. Praying in nature can remind us even more of the amazing and awesome God who spoke our world into existence. I would love to have been with these women in Thyatira who gathered regardless of their small number and outside forces, who pressed their way each week to a gathering place with their sisters. I'm sure they found strength and hope at their meeting, and on this particular day, God arranged for them to encounter Christ, as shared by Paul.

Paul and his companions stopped and talked to Lydia and the others in her group gathered for prayer at the river. How coincidental was this? These people happened to be at the same place Paul was allowed to go on this particular day and at this particular time. There weren't any bulletin boards announcing the time and place of their prayer meeting, but somehow Paul found some faithful women when he showed up at just this time.

I don't think many encounters are just happenstance. If we really believe God is guiding us and leading us and others, we will do well to take in each moment and let it shape us as we share what we have to shape others. So Lydia, who already believed in God, had her heart opened and her soil ripened for harvest. She hadn't yet accepted Jesus as savior, which was who Paul was speaking about. But because Lydia's heart was right, because she was in the right place at the right time, which was ordained by God, and because she was already on the path of worshiping God, her life was changed that day. She became a believer in Christ (Acts 16:14–15). No more rules and regulations and sacrifices.

A new covenant was established that day with Lydia. She became personally acquainted with the same Jesus who had cast out seven demons from Mary Magdalene (her label still follows), she accepted the man who had sat with Mary and Martha in Bethany, she understood who gave Priscilla her courage and strength, and she received the same Jesus who inspired Lois and Eunice to impart faith to a young Timothy. Down by the riverside, Lydia became a Christian that day and joined a band of women whose faith would change the world. What a day!

Oh Happy Day

Can you remember the day you believed, the day your life changed, your heart turned to God, and you received salvation? Do you remember the day your demons were cast out, your past was wiped out and forgiven, and you were made anew, the day you were made to love, made to forgive, made to share, made to live this way? Sometimes it is worth remembering that day or the chain of events leading to that day so you can recall your influence and power and use it for good, like Lydia did.

You see, Lydia didn't just receive Christ that day Paul happened to stop by; Lydia's entire household received Christ. The woman had influence. She was apparently a very successful businesswoman. She dealt with textiles and cloth and an expensive dye known as purple. (Even then people liked their clothes and homes to look pretty; Lydia evidently had the key to help them adorn their outward appearances well. And now she had the key to help them become beautiful from the inside out.) Lydia ran her household and influenced them as well. Every member of her household's life changed that day because her life changed. She had a domino effect on her family.

She probably had such a commanding presence and persuasive leadership qualities that everyone naturally did what she did. She didn't have to yell and scream to get them to follow; she just lived, and they naturally came after her. She was the one handling her business. She was the one taking care of business. She was a natural leader, and her household naturally followed her. Because of her decision that day, they too decided to accept Christ and follow his way. Real leaders rarely have to coerce followers; people are attracted to genuine leaders because of their sincerity, integrity, and dedication.

Is anyone following Christ because of you? How influential are you over your household? Are they happy when you are not home, or do they welcome you when you walk through the door? Has your nagging and prodding and fussing caused them to turn a deaf ear to your influence? Or does your life serve as a beacon, drawing them in closer to you?

Sometimes we think we have to coerce our family members to follow our decision to follow Christ. We want them to experience Christ as we have. Lydia's encounter with Paul reminds me that God is the master arranger of times and events. God knows when each person on my prayer list will submit to his will. God knows when each person in my line of influence will make a decision and fully embrace him—in the way that God sees fit, not in the way that I desire. Everyone's journey to Christ can take a different path. It's not up to me to set that course, but I can let my light shine and my life show who I follow. I know those close to me are watching and observing, and I know God sees and hears and has ordained an appointed time.

What I can do is use my resources in a way that honors God and advances the spreading of the Good News of Christ. I can be like Lydia and use my possessions—in her case, her home—to take care of others who may need help as they advance the message of the gospel. I know that what I have is really a gift from God, so I can return it to God through the ways I use my resources on earth.

When was the last time you used your home to host others who may or may not know Christ? When was the last time you used your home or other resources to offer a rest or retreat to those who labor sharing the gospel message or caring for the souls of others? What you do may influence others and create a domino effect, impacting others for years to come.

Hospitality That Matters

My conversion experience, what I consider as my full dedication to Christ, occurred in a home, not in a church. I was a freshman in college and I loved a good party, but I had nothing on my schedule one Saturday night. Instead of hanging in the dorm and playing cards (an old standby for broke college students), I agreed to tag along to a house party with another freshman friend. I didn't know much about the party, but I heard the word *party* and was game. I think someone picked us up and drove us to a home in suburban New Orleans. I recognized some of the faces at the party. I think the host was an upperclassman, and her parents allowed her to have the party in their home.

We played games, ate, and fellowshipped. It was fun. When no alcohol was served, I think I realized quickly that it was a Christian fellowship. Since I identified as a Christian and loved board games, I was able to have a great time without the alcoholic beverages. I think I had just as good a time as I probably had dancing at a club the night before. It was refreshing to be around young

Christians who partied at a home without smoking and alcohol.

But what I thought was a regular, clean, and wholesome party eventually changed into what would prompt my conversion experience. At the end of this party, we had prayer. We gathered in a circle and shared what we wanted to pray about. I sat quietly at first in my seat and began to reflect about my first year of college away from home and away from the watchful eyes of my parents. All throughout high school, I had been focused on doing exactly what my parents said just so I could make my escape and go away to college to do all the things I thought I wanted to do. I had successfully gotten past those high school years and my parents, and I was living on my own in college. I was doing what I thought I wanted to do with whomever I wanted to do it with. But as I sat in that circle, surrounded by college-aged Christians who were committed to living the Christian life, I reflected on that year.

In that moment, as I sat quietly, I realized that I was empty. I realized that the parties had not made me feel better. The relationships I had been in had not made me feel more desirable. The things I had done (which I would never tell my parents about) had really not been meaningful. While they may have been fun for a moment, I felt empty. I felt disconnected from God, and I felt alone. But right there in a prayer circle at a party in the home of Christians, a minister who also worked at the college asked if I wanted him to pray for me. I looked up with tears and shared that I hadn't lived as a Christian this year and I was sorry. His words have stayed with me throughout this journey. He said, "Katara, God has forgiven you. Now you have to forgive yourself."

I received the forgiveness of God immediately. I felt it and I reveled in it. I prayed for God to help me forgive myself—and most importantly, to help me follow the path he wanted me to be on. I knew that day that I needed to rid myself of some relationships and some habits, and I prayed about them. I know for a fact that my life was changed that day. I can look back at the time spent in the home of that family and know that that day their house was used to share the gospel; their resources were used to change at least one college freshman's life.

My journey would be filled with ups and downs after that life-changing day, but my hope and trust in God was cemented. I didn't live perfectly after that fellowship night, nor do I now, but I do live changed. I do live like God has forgiven me and I have forgiven myself. I do live in relationship with Jesus. I do pray and hope and wait. My life has changed, and I hope I've lived a life that changes others' lives—all because I had no other party to attend on a Saturday night back in 1989.

So, with my conversion story in my mind, I am reminded that I want to be more like Lydia. I want to use my home and my resources to show Christ to others. I want to be the professional businesswoman people respect and can count on to deliver the goods. After all, everyone wants to look beautiful. But, more important, I want to live in such a manner that those who come in contact with me want to know what drives me. They want to see what's making me calm and loving and generous and hopeful so they take a step closer, even when we're doing business. They are attracted to something inside of me. They may not be able to know what, but I trust in God's divine timing, and I know that our encounter is not in vain.

Come, let me show you some fabric and textiles that will make your home beautiful, but when you get here you're going to see even more. You're going to see a beautiful spirit and wonder what makes me tick. You're going to watch me more closely, and you may even ask a question. You're going to hear my tone and not be turned away. You're going to want to know more, and when the time is right, I will share with you the love I have, the joy I have, the peace I have.

You see, it's like no other. It's not something I can sell or manufacture. It comes from knowing God and loving Christ. It comes from forgiving myself and trusting God. It comes from taking my position as leader of my home and leader in the community seriously but not too seriously, because, after all, I really want to point you to Christ, the one who can change all things and make them beautiful.

Come, buy your cloth and find something more. I

know I've got that kind of influence, so I'm awaiting God's prompting to use it. I'm not taking my appointments for granted—because nothing happens by chance.

—

I am Lydia. I am good at what I do professionally. I use my God-given skills to lead well and work well. My personal and professional life reflects my love of God and trust in him. I am influential because of who I am and because of who I believe in. I don't have to preach it; I live it. My lifestyle reflects my commitment to Christ, and others want to follow him because of how I live. I open my home to others so that they may see Christ and feel his presence. I know that much of my evangelistic work is done outside of the church. Sometimes it's done in the workplace, sometimes it's done at home, and other times it is just right there in nature where I can cast my eyes on God's creation. My story follows me, and I am glad about it. I want others to know Christ as I do. He has changed my life.

Acknowledgments

As I reviewed the edits on my second book (wow!), I copied a few passages and e-mailed them to friends—making sure it was okay to include their stories as illustrations in the accounts of *Successful Women of the Bible*. Each gladly agreed to be included. Even though I don't provide their names, they each know who they are. I appreciate the journey we get to share, my friends.

I also sent a passage to Derrick, my husband; often we tell the same stories from different vantage points—and I've learned to appreciate that and him. Derrick, I love you and am so thankful we get to journey together. I always want to thank my daughter, Kayla, who puts up with Mommy's writing schedule. You are a delight to parent, Kayla. I will always thank God for blessing our family with you. I continue to give gratitude for my entire family and the influence you all have had on my life.

I always want to thank my Hachette/FaithWords family for their excellent work. Publishing is a giant team effort.

Thank you: Adrienne Ingrum, Grace Tweedy, Carolyn Kurek, Bob Castillo, JuLee Brand, Melissa Mathlin, and Lexi Smail.

And last but certainly not least, I am eternally grateful that God has smiled on me with the opportunity to write for a living.